THE
GOLDEN AGE
OF
TRAVEL
1880-1939

52

ALEXIS GREGORY

THE GOLDEN AGE OF TRAVEL

1880-1939

RIZZOLI
NEW YORK

First published in the United States of America in 1991
by RIZZOLI INTERNATIONAL PUBLICATIONS, INC.
300 Park Avenue South, New York, NY 10010

Copyright © 1990 by Société Nouvelle des Éditions
du Chêne
Text © 1990 Alexis Gregory

Library of Congress Cataloging-in-Publication Data
Gregory, Alexis
    The golden age of travel, 1850–1939 / Alexis Gregory.
      p.   cm.
    ISBN 0-8478-1250-2
    1. Voyages and travels.   I. Title.
G463.G765   1990
910.4 dc20
                                        90–52695
                                           CIP

Printed and bound in Italy

ISBN 0-8478-1250-2

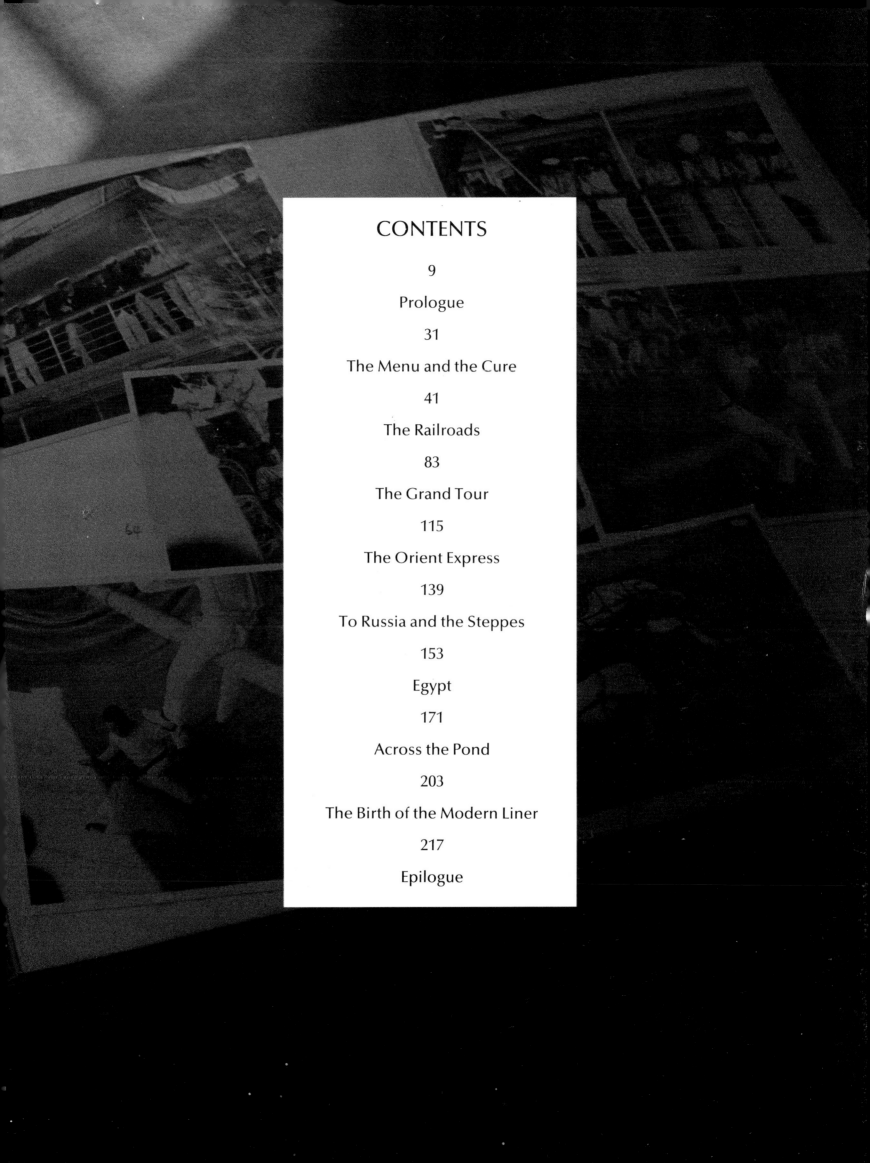

CONTENTS

PROLOGUE

By Water (Waiting at Dockside) 1881.

James Tissot. Owen Edgar Gallery, London.

Above The Prince of Wales arrives at

Cowes on *Osborne* in 1898.

There are endless reasons to temporarily leave the familiarity and comfort of home and endure the inevitable insecurity and anxiety that are always linked to the joys of a trip abroad; education, work, health, romance, hedonism, adventure, social interchange or mere curiosity. Until the middle of the nineteenth century, travel for pleasure was severely limited by a lack of roads and hotels, by wandering brigands and hundreds of different currencies and frontiers. People traveled only if they had to or, in the case of the exceedingly rich and idle British upper classes, if they had nothing better to do than wander around in the hope of becoming less parochial and consequently finer gentlemen. Then steam changed everything.

Steam powered the machines that created the newly rich industrial bourgeoisie, who wanted and indeed needed to spread the mercantile gospel throughout the world. Steam powered the newfangled trains that early observers feared were life-threatening (surely no one could survive speeds greater than ten miles per hour). Steam drove the pistons deep in the iron hulls of the largest ships the world had ever seen—and then poured through the turbines of even larger ships. It warmed radiators in vast new palace hotels where tropical palms could flourish even when ice caked the windows that looked onto great new boulevards, it drove the generators that lit up the glistening chandeliers of palaces and casinos.

Steam came from coal shoveled day and night by

sweating, dust-covered stokers maddened by their long exposure to nearly unbearable flames. Aboard the new, luxurious liners crossing the Atlantic, passengers were cosseted in inconceivable luxury while the black gang below never saw the light of day. Wagner's *Nibelungen* were the symbol of the day, crawling underground, whipped on by a greedy Alberich whose gold brought only misfortune and tragedy.

This book covers a period of less than a century, from the mid-nineteenth century up to the cataclysm of World War II, which dealt the death blow to a crumbling aristocracy and an indifferent plutocracy. Income tax and inheritance taxes did their bit as well; both were based on the theory that earned income should be encouraged and unearned, inherited wealth confiscated. This golden age of travel was enjoyed by men of great stature and wealth and ladies of frivolity and breeding. It was an age of optimism in which titanic figures rode waves of vast new wealth: Henry Ford, whose Model T forced governments to build roads and highways; J. P. Morgan and Otto Kahn, who financed railroads and shipping on a worldwide scale; Sir Henri Deterding, who was the director-general of Royal Dutch Shell; Thomas Edison, who lit up the world; and Alexander Graham Bell, who wired it together. Travel owes the Cook's tour to Thomas Cook, the ritzy life to César Ritz, and the Pullman car to George Pullman. This book is largely devoted to them and other pioneers, and to the great travelers whose demands they satisfied. They were tough, single-minded, and often cruel—and they had style. And style, after all, is the stuff of legend.

THE EDWARDIANS

When Richard D'Oyly Carte offered César Ritz a king's ransom to come to London and run the Savoy Hotel, the great palace on the Thames Embankment that he had begun building in the late 1880s, the wily Ritz knew exactly what the impresario wanted. He told his wife, Marie Louise, when both were busily making Baden-Baden into the elegant resort it quickly became: "He wants the clientele I can give him, the people who come here, who go to Baden, who were my

The industrial revolution gave birth to many new inventions that completely

changed the face of travel. The luxury of the age—for a lucky few—also depended

on a large force of available and underpriced labor. *Left* Henry Ford is seen

with his earliest and latest Model T, celebrating the 10,000,000th car to

roll off his assembly line. *Right* A steamfitter, as photographed by Lewis W. Hine

in 1920. Steam was the driving force of the period.

patrons at Lucerne and Monte Carlo: the Marlborough House set—Lord Rosebery, Lord and Lady Elch, Lord and Lady Gosford, Lord and Lady de Grey, and the Sassoons; the Roman princes, Rudini, the Crespis, the Rospigliosis; the Radziwills, and so forth; the best of theatre and opera crowd—Patti, the de Reszkes, Coquelin, Bernhardt; the Grand Dukes and the smart Parisian crowd—the Castellanes, the Breteuils, the Sagans; he wants the Vanderbilts and Morgans; he wants the Rothschilds."

At the very thought Ritz fell into a fit of exhaustion, and Marie Louise had to play Gounod's "Ave Maria" on the piano to calm him.

There were others Ritz could have added. Above all, ruling international society with an unusual combina-

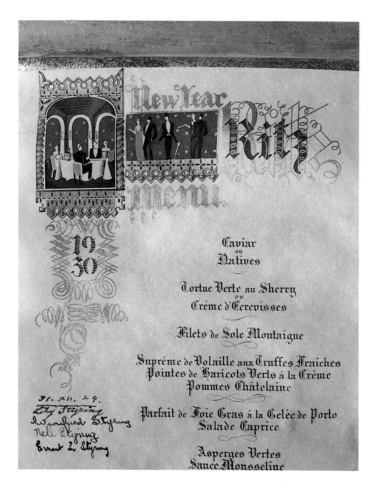

tion of bonhomie, grandeur, and sensuality was the bearded Hanoverian Prince of Wales—Bertie, later Edward VII. Bertie was a sustaining breath of air in Victorian England. While "Mama" carried on her hypocritical affair with John Brown, though always dressed in widow's weeds in mourning for the late Prince Albert, Bertie toured the fleshpots of Europe, ordered gluttonous meals at Maxim's and Voisin, and then retired upstairs to the *chambres privées* with one of Paris's legendary cocottes, known appropriately as *les grandes horizontales*. In a wonderful upstairs-downstairs vignette of the period, the younger waiters at Voisin were apprehended drilling peepholes into a love nest's door, curious to know whether princes made love like ordinary mortals. They might have seen La Païva happily intertwined with a Russian grand duke, Liane de Pougy arousing a visiting head of state, or Emilienne d'Alençon soothing the nerves of an American tycoon. De Pougy, one of the greatest of the easy beauties, complimented Ritz in his later years: "You can lay down the law now, for you have reached the height of your career in your profession—as I have, in mine." "Alas," said Ritz, "I am afraid with far less pleasure and far more trouble than you have experienced, Mademoiselle."

In his list, Ritz could also have mentioned the appallingly rich and self-indulgent Indian maharajas who, thanks to the P&O Line, could now lavish their splendor on dazzled Europeans. When the Maharaja of Bikaner came to London, he took over an entire floor of Ritz's establishment on Piccadilly—and he needed it! A maharaja traveled with his prime minister and his suite, aides-de-camp, private secretaries, bearers, several wives from the zenana (with *their* servants), cooks, children (each with German and British nannies *and* their ayahs), bodyguards, and, presumably, porters for their chests of precious jewels.

The Maharaja of Jaipur took abroad giant silver urns of Ganges water, enough for a year of ablutions, and his son later traveled with strings of polo ponies. The Indian princes came officially to render homage to their Queen Empress Victoria, a delicate matter since as a widow she was theoretically an untouchable.

They also came to shop. Cartier's windows were emptied, as were Asprey's; entire floors of Maples

César Ritz (*inset*) and Thomas Cook were among the greatest innovators of modern travel. Ritz created a standard of comfort for the beau monde which has never been paralleled, and with the help of the legendary Escoffier, brought magnificent food into his establishments. Together, they reduced the gargantuan menu to a manageable selection of dishes, as can be seen above. Thomas Cook's magazine The Excursionist, for which an advertisement appears opposite, described his tours and was the first travel magazine ever published.

WHITSUNTIDE NUMBER.

Established 1851.   Vol. LII.   No. 4.—MAY 3. 1902.   Price 2d. By Post 4d.

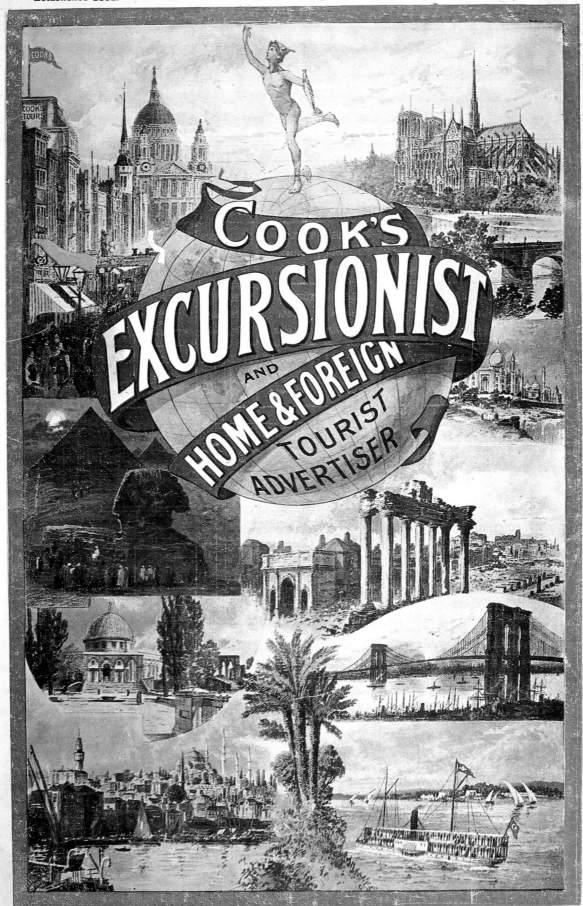

Cook's EXCURSIONIST AND HOME & FOREIGN TOURIST ADVERTISER

Johnson, Riddle, Couchman & Co., Southwark Bridge Road, S.E.

THOS. COOK & SON, CHIEF OFFICE, LUDGATE CIRCUS, LONDON.

furniture were crated up to fill their new palaces and give them a fashionable Western look. Gigantic crystal chandeliers were ordered at Baccarat, as were suites of glass furniture. The Maharaja of Kapurthala, a fixture in Paris society, ordered copies of French eighteenth-century furniture for a jungle folly modeled on Versailles, and the Maharaja of Indore commissioned Art Deco *ensemblier* Emile-Jacques Ruhlmann to design a pavilion, priceless furniture to fill it, and a private railroad car.

Ritz also could have mentioned the Russian nobles and merchant princes who rode the night trains to Paris and Nice—where they had villas, kept mistresses, and gambled away fortunes—and the stars of the Ballets Russes: Sergei Diaghilev, Vaslav Nijinsky, and Léon Bakst.

Most important to the renown of his hotels were the royals, always in perpetual motion, moving from coronations to funerals, from christenings to engagement balls. There were flocks of them. At the turn of the century, and particularly before Bismarck unified Germany, endless sets of princes and kings sat on often shaky thrones from small Teutonic states to the jungles of Brazil.

All these were the gilded travelers on an endless round of pleasure. For the privileged few, life could be characterized as a nonstop exchange program of the rich of all nations.

In the cold weather, one went to the seaside—southern Italy or the Riviera. Queen Victoria was often found at Cimiez, the Prince of Wales in Monte Carlo, and the English grandees on Nice's Promenade des Anglais. From Christmas to Lent there was the enchanting round of the Saint Petersburg season. The more adventurous wintered in India or Egypt, taking the sun on the tented terrace of the Cataract Hotel in Aswan or luxuriating at Shepheard's in Cairo, which was the center of an incredibly opulent social life in which beys and pashas filled the napkins of their European guests with gold and jeweled souvenirs. Spring and early summer were the social seasons of Paris, London, and Vienna. In mid-summer there were the spas—Baden-Baden, Carlsbad, Bad Homburg, Montecatini, and Vichy—or the mountain resorts of Switzerland and the Alto Adige. Fall brought shoots on the

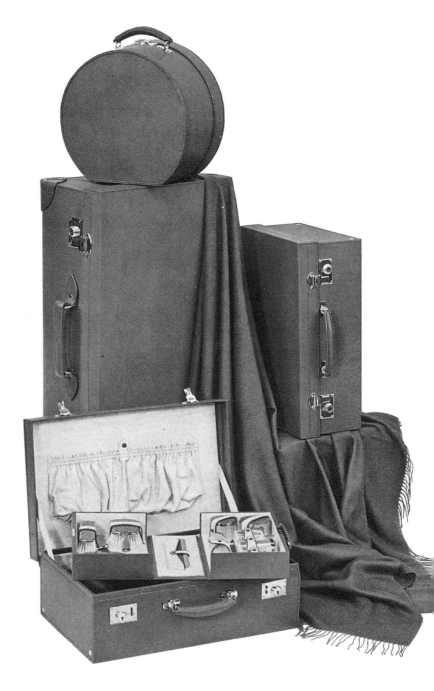

Above **A selection of luggage from Asprey's, including a gentleman's toilet case and a lady's hat box. This would have been merely a fraction of the baggage needed to keep a well-dressed couple in the latest fashion at an elegant resort.**

great estates of Britain, France, and Austria-Hungary. "My whole life is a season," complained a fashionable Edwardian gentleman.

THE LONDON SEASON AND THE TRAVELER

Leading the dance were the English, and not only because of the cosmopolitan Bertie. Great Britain led the Industrial Revolution; her colonies contributed staggering wealth; her banking system was the clearinghouse of world trade. A buyer of equipment in Japan would open a letter of credit on behalf of the seller in Silesia in a British bank in pounds sterling; both would have felt insecure with any other arrangement. Great loans were floated by Barings and the British Rothschilds, national debt was denominated in sterling; even the mighty Romanovs kept their nest egg in London. Britain's bankers combined the discretion

Above A poster from the beginning of the century praises the lines of the two largest French shipping companies, while the flags of the countries they served flutter on each of the masts. Until the opening of the Panama Canal in August 1914, a trip around the world also entailed a train journey across the continent of America.

and efficiency of Zurich's Bahnhofstrasse with the vast scope of today's Wall Street. The dollar was an esoteric currency, and Switzerland was used only for rest cures.

Britain was practically always the first port of call for the newly rich Americans. They could speak the language, and many of Britain's great families welcomed an infusion of cash. Even the Prince of Wales made a point of cultivating the rich: American, South African, and Jewish magnates were among his closest friends and advisers. The Astors became British lords, and Consuelo Vanderbilt became the ninth duchess of Marlborough, thanks to a dowry of £2,000,000 at a time when a nice town house could be rented for £60 a year. The trappings of the Roxburgh Graces were bought with a little less, but Jay Gould broke the record in selling his daughter to Count Boni de Castellane for £3,000,000. Presumably, the fussier French aristocracy felt that they would settle only for a higher price.

Many eligible gentlemen living on small incomes waited eagerly for heiresses to step off a liner and check into London's Carlton or Ritz. The great migration of America's rich started when the blossoms fell in Central Park and the first summer heat penetrated the walls of the imitation châteaus and palazzi on Fifth Avenue. It flowed in the opposite direction (as it still does today) when New England's schools and colleges reopened in September. Notwithstanding, many of the girls were destined for finishing schools run by impoverished aristocratic ladies, particularly in Florence and Dresden (Switzerland, again, would come later), and many of the boys stayed on in London or Frankfurt to develop the business acumen and contacts necessary for their fathers' empires. Parents generally accompanied their offspring, guided their social and intellectual development, and were ever on the lookout for a good match.

For the gilded American traveler, the trip to Europe would start when the chauffeur brought the car to the front door. Next to him was the footman to assist the family. Luggage was trucked to the pier—giant steamer trunks packed for the endless balls, country weekends, Royal Ascot and Henley, parading in Europe's resorts, and even, possibly, for presentation at court. For a country weekend, everybody took along a mountain of luggage. Lady Cynthia Asquith remembered coming to breakfast in her "best dress," usually of velvet, changing into tweeds after church, and then putting on a seductive tea gown before retiring upstairs to change into full evening dress. Thus, a weekend involved the "Sunday best," two tweed coats and skirts, three tea dresses, and two important evening gowns, not to mention petticoats, overcoats, stoles, hats, scarves, day and evening bags, and feather boas. The men needed brightly colored velvet smoking suits for tea, tweeds for shooting, a dark suit for church, white tie and tails, and innumerable pieces of headgear. No wonder a rich man traveled with his valet, while his wife took along her maid.

Great nets hauled the baggage marked "Not Wanted on the Voyage" into the ship's hold, leaving aside a trunk or two needed for the crossing. The large Louis Vuitton pieces, purchased in New York or Paris, split down the middle to reveal suits and dresses hung

---

The Prince of Wales (*above*), poses in front on a tender on one of his many trips to the United States. A great fashion plate,

HRH traveled in society with the likes of Lady Cunard (posing, opposite, at a ball at the Hotel Savoy in London alongside the

Maharaja of Alwar). Emerald Cunard's flat on Grosvenor Square was a gathering place for London's café

society, and her open support of the romance of the Prince with Wallis Simpson—not to speak of her intimate power dinners

for Hitler's British ambassador (and later Foreign Secretary) von Ribbentrop—put her in bad odor with Britain's

establishment.

straight and drawers full of linens. Upon arrival in Southampton or Cherbourg, a porter from Claridge's or the Ritz fetched the luggage at the pier—VIP luggage was unloaded first—and rushed on ahead to get it into the suite before the guests arrived. The London trunk would be unpacked by the hotel's maid and valet; the rest—labeled "Paris," "Karlsbad," or "Venice" —would be stacked in the corridor. In season, when the great hotels and their storerooms were filled, the corridors resembled obstacle courses, even though they were designed with such impediments in mind. (The designers did not, however, anticipate the Indian servants who invariably camped out, fully dressed, at their master's door when he retired for the night.)

Today's hotel guest would immediately reach for a touch-tone telephone to arrange his schedule. Not in Edwardian England. One called on one's friends between three and six P.M. If the lady of the house was not "at home," the visitor gave the servant two of her cards, each with a corner turned down to indicate that she had "left cards" in person. The lady of the house would then send her carriage to deliver an engraved invitation to one of the endless receptions that made up the London season. To save time and useless calls, one interviewed the hall porter, who—with the ingrained snobbism of all good servants—kept tabs on the aristocracy. "The Duke and Duchess of Marlborough left for Paris yesterday, Madame. They will return Wednesday." "Lord Rothschild is in Frankfurt, Sir, and his return is uncertain." "The Prince of Hesse has left suddenly yesterday for Her Royal Highness's funeral."

Not every visitor, even if extremely rich, had the key to London's social life. Only so many foreigners were allowed into a very closed circle, and there were others who had no interest in participating. For them, London still had endless delights—splendid theaters, opera, cafés, shopping, and museums. And, of course, there were still people who worked for a living. For them, Henley and Royal Ascot were tribal performances.

Changing clothes was an absolute obsession in the Belle Epoque, and no lady or gentlemen could possibly travel without a personal maid or valet to unpack, press and lay out the various changes of dress needed at different times of day. A maid (*above*) packs somewhat light clothes in a steamer trunk. In London (*below right*) even an ordinary dinner for two at a hotel required the gentleman to arrive in white tie and tails and his date in a long evening dress and jewels.

Sea crossings, during which there was little to do, encouraged non-stop dressing. There were tweeds for the gentlemen and flannel skirts for the ladies in the morning, suits and silk dresses for lunch, diaphanous velvet tea gowns for the later afternoon and full evening dress except for the first and last nights which were spent unpacking and repacking the large Vuitton steamer trunks. The best gowns and jewels were brought out for the Captain's dinner at which gentlemen regularly wore their decorations, particularly if invited to the skipper's table. Life on the CGT *La Provence* followed the rituals, as can be seen in these watercolors by E. Louis Lessieux.

COWES

The greatest of these was the Cowes Regatta, which wound up the season.

In the last year of King Edward's reign, a vast fleet of yachts gathered for Cowes Regatta. The *Victoria and Albert*, with her attendant battleship, dominated the roadstead. The Tzar come in his yacht *Standart*, the Kaiser in the *Hohenzollern*, and the King of Spain with his racing yacht *Hispania*. All three presented prizes. The King entertained twenty members of the R.Y.S. to dinner aboard the *Victoria and Albert* to be presented to the Tzar. Ashore and afloat there were dinner parties and balls. Steam launches, with gleaming brass funnels, and slender cutters and gigs, pulled by their crews at the long white oars, plied between the yachts and the Squadron steps. By day, the sails of the racing yachts spread across the blue waters of the Solent like the wings of giant butterflies, by night the riding lights and lanterns gleamed and shone like glow-worms against the onyx waters and fireworks burst and spent themselves in the night sky. And over this splendid scene presided the King—a genial, portly, yet always majestic figure.

There has never been a regatta as glamorous as

Cowes at the end of the last century, thanks to the Prince of Wales. Bertie, elected Commodore of the Royal Yacht Squadron in 1882, was omnipresent, moving from one great yacht to the other, parading on the squadron's lawns in naval uniform that was regulation—save for the beauty hanging on his arm and his large Havana cigar. Wherever else important yachtsmen went the rest of the year, they invariably ended up at Cowes in August. So did many monarchs—the kaiser, the Austrian emperor, the czar of Russia, Empress Eugénie of France. Even the Vatican felt the pressure to participate, hence the blazing white *Immacolata Concezione* commissioned for Pope Leo XIII. England's nobles steamed or sailed in, as did America's tycoons, whose yachts resembled ocean liners.

The pretext was sailing, and the Solent was filled with bobbing masts, flags, and graceful sloops. The star racers were Sir Thomas Lipton aboard the *Shamrock*, the first of his five America's Cup challengers (all of them unsuccessful, except at generating publicity) and Bertie aboard his *Britannia*, which was fast enough to win and, at 122 feet, roomy enough to accommodate the sybaritic prince in comfort. The Queen's yacht was the more sedate *Victoria and Albert II*, built in 1855. She was 300 feet long, had twelve cabins for the eighteen members of the royal household, and a crew of 240. There were two tea houses, a chapel, a nursery, sumptuous apartments for the Queen and Prince Albert, and small drawing rooms as well as large rooms for the business of state. For all that, Victoria herself was seldom afloat. After Prince Albert's death in 1860, the beautiful ship was put at the disposition of her son.

Kaiser Wilhelm was invited to join the Royal Squadron in 1889. Bertie later complained that "the regatta used to be my favourite relaxation; but since the Emperor has been in command here, it's nothing but a nuisance." The arrogant monarch felt obliged to outdo his British cousins; they in turn considered him a dreadful boor. He commissioned the *Hohenzollern*, a 383-foot destroyer painted white and garnished with a gold imperial eagle. Utterly without style, she looked oafish among the sleek and graceful yachts around her. The kaiser even tried to steal Cowes' glamour by

The restaurant at Claridge's, on Upper Brook Street, was one of the many

fashionable places to dine in London, and has always been the favorite

hotel for British and European royalty. *Opposite* A special Vuitton trunk

built to carry ladies' hats in protective cages.

organizing his own regatta at Kiel, but at first just rich Americans came. It had no cachet until 1904, when Bertie, by then Edward VII, asked his yachting pals to join him there.

Of all the royal yachts, the most beautiful was the czar's 420-foot, 4,500-ton *Standart*, which was the imperial family's favorite retreat. Every June they spent two weeks cruising the rocky Finnish coast, mooring in deserted coves and picnicking or exploring ashore. Many a landowner was flabbergasted to find the czar at his door, politely asking whether he and his family might use the tennis court. Despite the relaxed atmosphere, the *Standart* was usually accompanied at Cowes by torpedo boats and dispatch vessels carrying state papers from Saint Petersburg. It was from the decks of the lovely *Standart*, in 1909, that the imperial family had its last look at England. Her crew lined the

Magnificent yachts were an essential appurtenance of Europe's royal families—floating palaces on which they sought privacy, negotiated treaties, reflected national pride and grandeur, and received each other in the style to which they were accustomed. *Above* Officers dining on the stern of the Kaiser's *Hohenzollern*. *Below* The grandest of all royal yachts, the *Britannia*, travels to review the fleet at Spithead in 1911. *Opposite* The smaller *Surprise*, the yacht of the Duke of Edinburgh in Barcelona in 1888. *Overleaf* "The Ball on Shipboard" *c.*1874 by James Tissot. Tate Gallery, London. This magnificent reflection of *fin-de-siècle* shipboard opulence is a total fantasy of the artist, but the brilliant display of flags and massed sailors in the background were certainly inspired by the Naval Review at Cowes.

deck as the czar reviewed the Royal Navy off the Isle of Wight. Bands played "God Save the Czar" and "God Save the King," and British seamen cheered. In 1912, the czar and the kaiser met for the last time when the *Standart* and the *Hohenzollern* anchored side by side at Revel (now Tallinn) on the Baltic. There was an attempt to patch up differences, but it was too late. A few years later, the *Standart* became a Soviet minelayer, the *Hohenzollern* was scrapped, and cataclysm had toppled both the monarchs and their empires.

After the regatta the court retired to Balmoral, the aristocracy returned to killing birds, and London's gilded visitors, with their great steamer trunks, moved on.

YANKEE SPLENDOR

At Cowes and elsewhere, leading members of the New York Yacht Club were also capable of cutting glamorous figures. Barons of industry, finance, and commerce wanted to rub shoulders with the swells of Europe, and the swells were delighted to inspect their yachts. The kaiser, on a visit to Morton F. Planck's schooner *Ingomar* at Kiel, muttered as he signed the guest book "Dear, dear, even a silver book. How rich you Americans are." We have no record of his visiting William Vanderbilt's *Alva*, Anthony Drexel's *Margarita*, James Gordon Bennett's *Jeanette*, *Namouna* or *Lysistrata*, or—grandest of all—one of J. P. Morgan's four *Corsairs*, any one of which made the *Ingomar* look like a launch. He would probably have declared war on the spot out of sheer envy.

The first American superyacht was Commodore Cornelius Vanderbilt's famous *North Star*, a 270-foot paddle steamer that first crossed the Atlantic in 1853. In every respect she was a full-fledged ocean liner, filled with Louis XV chairs, period fireplaces, and a sofa for twenty people. The dining room was paneled in marble and granite; its painted ceiling was decorated with heroes of the New World. Vanderbilt traveled with his family and friends, as well as his personal physician and chaplain and *their* wives, in ten large staterooms. His first port of call was the Isle of Wight, where the thousands who greeted the fabulous ship were invited aboard to marvel at her. A newspaper was inspired to write that "it is time that *parvenu* should be looked on as a word of honour." The *North Star* paddled on to Saint Petersburg, and shortly afterward a jealous Czar Alexander III ordered his own paddle steamer.

James Gordon Bennett, a newspaper owner who, among other things, sent Stanley off to find Livingstone, was the first to surpass the commodore at sea. The last of his three yachts, the *Lysistrata*, was 314 feet long, so spacious that Bennett had a suite on each of her three decks. There was a crew of a hundred, a Turkish bath, and a cow in a padded cell to supply fresh milk. To nobody's surprise, Bennett died broke after squandering a fortune of $40,000,000.

By the end of the century, the luxury yacht had become something of a stereotype: long, lean hull, smart clipper bow, one tall, thin funnel, an elegantly

Above The Duke of York (later King George V) poses on board the royal yacht *Osborne* in 1877. The sons of Britain's monarchs all underwent a training course in the navy, although in far more comfortable conditions than their contemporaries. Naval uniform, or variations thereon, were standard gear for all royal children. *Opposite* Félix Faure, the President of France, with the Emperor Nicolas II on the royal Russian yacht *Standart* during the President's visit to Russia in 1899 when the historic Franco-Russian alliance was conceived. The full dress uniform of the heads of state reflects the importance of the occasion. The yacht was the only place where the Imperial Family could totally escape from the stifling protocol that surrounded them.

shaped counter-projecting stern, two masts for auxiliary sails, and the interior decor of the country house. The yachts had antique furniture, fine paneling, thick carpets, marble fireplaces, and bedrooms out of the Ritz; sybaritic, sleek, imposing, and expensive, each was an extension of the rich man's house.

The century closed with the *Victoria and Albert III*, her crew of 367 supplemented by forty servants from Buckingham Palace when Edward VII and Queen Alexandra were aboard. During World War I, many great yachts were mobilized for U-boat patrols; some were sunk and others, worn out, were later scrapped. But in the euphoric 1920s, American millionaires built more fabulous ships, with gymnasiums, swimming pools, movie theaters, and—a major attraction during prohibition—bars, where owners and guests could tipple once beyond the three-mile limit. The most beautiful postwar yacht was Marjorie Merriweather Post's *Hussar*, a three-masted sailing ship that flew over the water on 35,822 square feet of sail. Built in 1931, during the depths of the Depression, the *Hussar* was filled with the customary priceless antiques and marble baths. When Mrs. Post married Joseph Davies in 1935, she changed the ship's name to *Sea Cloud* and took her to Leningrad when her husband was appointed ambassador to the Soviet Union. In the middle of Stalin's purge trials, as trainloads of the condemned left for Siberia and thousands starved, Mrs. Post bought up imperial treasures for a song and spirited them away aboard her floating palace. Wealth had its privileges even in Communist Russia, thanks in this case to a breakfast cereal called Post Toasties.

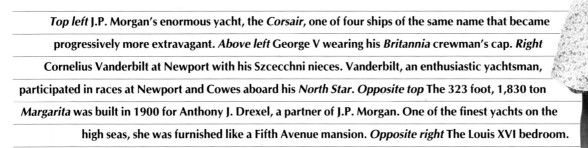

Top left J.P. Morgan's enormous yacht, the *Corsair*, one of four ships of the same name that became progressively more extravagant. *Above left* George V wearing his *Britannia* crewman's cap. *Right* Cornelius Vanderbilt at Newport with his Szcecchni nieces. Vanderbilt, an enthusiastic yachtsman, participated in races at Newport and Cowes aboard his *North Star*. *Opposite top* The 323 foot, 1,830 ton *Margarita* was built in 1900 for Anthony J. Drexel, a partner of J.P. Morgan. One of the finest yachts on the high seas, she was furnished like a Fifth Avenue mansion. *Opposite right* The Louis XVI bedroom.

THE MENU AND THE CURE

Opposite One of the

pump room refreshment bars at the

spa of Evian, painted in 1914.

ood played an extraordinarily important role in the life of the Edwardian beau monde. The gluttonous and portly Prince of Wales inspired his peers to create the most astonishing menus. Today one selects three courses from the lavish menu of a first-class restaurant, but until World War I a guest in a large country house or at a celebration in a luxury hotel or restaurant would stagger through a meal resembling an entire menu, organized according to a formula as strict as society protocol. Whether dinners were served at Buckingham Palace, Shepheard's in Cairo, the Taj in Bombay, or the Astoria in Saint Petersburg, its scenario was always written in French. If commercial transactions all bore the stamp of the British Empire, France ruled the stoves of the civilized world. The great Antonin Carême had set the style, moving from the Russian court to the Paris house of Baron James de Rothschild, the founder of the French branch of the banking family. Baron James counted Napoleon III and the Empress Eugénie among his intimates and engaged Chopin to play in his salon and Ingres to paint his beautiful wife, Baroness Betty, and for him Carême not only created great menus and dishes but literally *built* them: sweets often consisted of large *Temples d'Amour*, glazed pyramids, and other follies. Following quickly in Carême's tracks was the great Auguste Escoffier, who simplified the menu (up to a point, anyway), did away with Carême's construc-

tion projects, and became the key to the success of Ritz's hotels.

A precoronation banquet menu from Buckingham Palace, dated June 23, 1902, is quite typical of the times.

..MENU..

- - - - - -

Consommé Printainer à l'Impériale.
Consommé froid à l'Indienne.

- -

Blanchailles au Naturel et à la Diable.
Filets de Truites à la Russe.

- -

Cotelettes de Cailles à la Clamart.
Poulardes à la Norvégienne.

- -

Selles de Presalé à la Niçoise.
Jambon d'Espagne à la Basque.

- -

Ortolans rôtis sur Canapés.
Salade des quatre Saisons.

- -

Asperges froides à la Vinaigrette.

- -

Gâteau Punch granit au Champagne.
Gradins de Pâtisseries.

- -

Canapés d'Anchois à la Provençale.

- -

Petits Soufflés Glaces Princesse.
Gaufrettes.

BUCKINGHAM PALACE,
23 Juin, 1902.

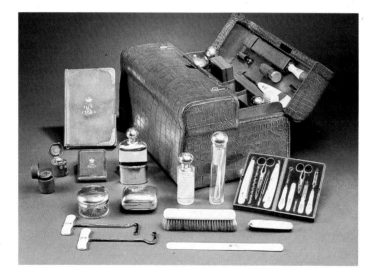

Edward VII was the very epitome of the spoiled and fun-loving golden traveler of the Belle Epoque. In what must have seemed an endless wait for Queen Victoria to die, he wandered through the resorts and capitals of Europe working his way through such endless and gargantuan meals as that listed above, and recuperating from his excesses in such spas as Marienbad, where he is seen opposite drinking mineral water and spreading his bonhomie among fellow *curistes*. The Prince's patronage of a resort, hotel or restaurant assured its long-lasting success. *Above* The Prince's silver-mounted crocodile dressing case.

The asparagus on the menu brings to mind a diplomatic incident at Windsor superbly resolved by Queen Victoria. At a banquet for the Shah of Iran, His Majesty was served asparagus. According to the custom of his Empire, he threw the uneaten stalk over his shoulder. To avoid embarrassment to her guest, the Queen followed suit and her bold gesture was instantly followed by the entire table as liveried footmen ducked the flying vegetables. Considering this precoronation menu,

it is not surprising that Bertie was taken ill, operated on for appendicitis, and missed his coronation as Edward VII, scheduled for three days later.

Gluttony was also satisfied at breakfast, lunch, and tea, with snacks and sweets consumed in between. A breakfast buffet at a country-house weekend would display in silver chafing dishes poached, boiled, and fried eggs, bacon, kedgeree, lamb chops, sausages, kidneys, porridge, grilled mackerel and turbot, fried

A menu of 1897, to commemorate the horse races that still take place yearly in Baden-Baden. The Victorian borders are sprinkled with flowers, and the fare is rather modest for the period, perhaps reflecting the diminished calorie intake of the *curistes*. Horse racing was one of the highlights of the Baden-Baden season, which drew the rich from all over Germany as well as the rest of Europe. Gains at the races were easily lost at the beautiful imitation rococo casino, a creation of Jacques Bénazet. Otherwise, days were spent walking in the lovely parks, in the Black Forest, or taking the waters.

sole, kippers, bloaters, and, naturally, toast, scones, and fruit in season. At Waddesdon Manor, the more continental Rothschilds served breakfast to guests in their rooms. "Tea or coffee, Madame?" "Tea, please." "China, jasmine, or black, Madame? Lemon, cream, or milk?" "Very well, Madame. Hertfordshire or Staffordshire cream?"

The breakfast menu of a Cunard liner, through the end of transatlantic travel in the sixties, was inspired by these Edwardian feasts, and the legendary menus the French Line offered on the sublime *Ile de France*, *Normandie*, *Liberté*, and *France* bore the stamp of Carême and Escoffier to the end. If the truth must be told, however, the gastronomic adventurer is better satisfied today, as the culinary lingua franca of the

Belle Epoque varied little from London to Bombay, and local specialties were generally considered food for peasants, not for the gilded traveler.

THE WATERS

After a winter of feasting and a spring of gluttony, it is no wonder that the rich and privileged felt slightly bilious. Blood pressures had risen, livers reeled, ladies had the vapors, and gentlemen no longer fit into their suits. Early August was the time to go to the spas of Austria, Germany, France, and Czechoslovakia for the curing effects of mineral water—imbibed, absorbed through the pores, or driven into the body by high-

Above Cure-takers in Wiesbaden at the turn of the century with glasses of mineral water in hand. The ritual of slowly imbibing water from mineral sources while resting to the sound of a string orchestra or promenading was probably as beneficial as the magic potion. *Inset* The legendary August Escoffier (1846–1935) whose magnificent culinary confections were responsible for many a bilious disposition. Escoffier, the close collaborator of César Ritz, worked with the latter at his Restaurant de la Conversation in Baden-Baden.

pressure hoses. Some spas specialized: Vichy was good for the liver, Evian for the kidneys, Bath for the skin, Bad Gastein for the hormonal system (since its radium woke up exhausted sexual drives), Karlsbad for stomach disorders, and so forth. The almighty spa doctor prescribed the correct dosage of water, a diet, and occasionally a regimen of exercise. Orchestras played as curists slowly drank one foul-tasting glass of mineral water after another, and strong-armed attendants buried their victims in radioactive mud and then beat them to within an inch of their lives before scraping them off with rough gloves.

The British could simply go from London to Brighton, where only sea water and bathing were prescribed. George IV, as Prince Regent, was responsible for transforming this small fishing village into a sublime Regency town. John Nash designed its Pavilion, decorated with minarets and domes, which in 1822 was the most dazzling folly of its time. It is still filled with dragons and serpents and every other wonder of the chinoiserie style, but much of its furniture has been moved to Buckingham Palace. Queen Victoria went to Brighton, and an absolutely splendid Pullman train —the first train de luxe to operate in Europe—made the 82 kilometer run as of December 5, 1881. There were four Pullman cars in the train, called Louise, Maud, Victoria and Beatrice, complete with incandescent bulbs, a drawing car for the ladies and a smoking car for the gents. This service lasted 91 years, but Brighton was abandoned by Queen Victoria and never adopted by her descendents. If the truth must be known, a monarch's patronage was probably more important to the success of a spa than the efficacity of its waters.

Edward VII, as prince and king, was true to his Hanoverian origins, and traveled yearly to Bad Homburg. He also liked Marienbad and set up summer court in Biarritz, where the Empress Eugénie had once reigned from a red-and-white palace, now rebuilt into the Hôtel du Palais. In Bad Homburg, the prince took the cure seriously, losing up to forty pounds on every visit. He arrived with numerous friends, who breakfasted with champagne at the Café Brahe, picnicked in the forests, and finished the nights at the Casino Restaurant. Wales adopted and adapted the hat of the

local militia, making the homburg an essential item of every gentleman's wardrobe. Bad Homburg was a suburb for rich bankers from Frankfurt, only ten miles away. Its beautiful Kurpark and Kurhaus were the creation of François Blanc, as was its large baroque casino. Blanc was to casinos what Ritz was to the grand hotel, and—as with Ritz—celebrities followed in his wake. King Chulalongkorn of Siam, Czar Nicholas II, Prince Lucien Bonaparte, and Kaiser Wilhelm II, as well as the kings of Sweden, Greece, and Bulgaria, all frequented Bad Homburg, as did German industrialists and American millionaires. Louis Blanc impoverished

A water massage at the Etablissement Thermale at Aix-les-Bains resembles some sort of medieval torture. Pushing water through the pores under immense pressure is supposed to add to the benefits acquired by imbibing it at other times of day.

both king and commoner at his resort, but they always came back.

BADEN-BADEN

The other still-fashionable German spa that was launched at the end of the last century is Baden-Baden, in the Black Forest. There is a Baden near Vienna and another near Zurich, but these are mere gleams of light next to the brilliance of this resort on the Rhine's east bank. The Romans discovered the thermal springs here—they are the hottest in Europe—and Caracalla laid out the original baths himself some two thousand years ago. The Friedrichsbad, where the curists flock, looks like a Central European parliament, and the water is supposed to cure arthritis, neuralgia, and respiratory diseases. The real cure, however, is the rest that comes from walking on the banks of the meandering, shallow Oos or on the manicured Lichtentaler Allee, lined with ancient and exotic trees. It was in Baden-Baden that Brahms wrote the Lichtenthal Symphony, and that Dostoevski and Turgenev spent the summer. "Come to Baden-Baden," Turgenev later wrote Flaubert, "there are trees here such as I've never seen elsewhere." Trees, however, were not sufficient diversion for the beau monde, who needed great hotels, a casino, society, and lavish restaurants. With Queen Victoria in residence at a modest pension, Kaiser Wilhem I and the Kaiserin Augusta at the Maison Messmer, Napoleon III at the Villa Stephanie, and the emperor of Brazil, Dom Pedro II, Bismarck, and King Alfonso XIII scattered among other hostelries, there was no problem in attracting a rich clientele. It quickly became fashionable for Russians to own a villa here, and their palaces are still standing today—mostly as pensions for less affluent travelers.

Baden-Baden has what may be the most delightful casino in Europe: it gave Monte Carlo a run for its money until Germany prohibited gambling in 1870. Reopened during World War II, the casino was the creation of Jacques Bénazet and his son Edouard, who commissioned a winter garden, ballrooms in the style of the French monarchs, and an exquisite little

theater that attracted famous performers. The Bénazets also built a track nearby at Iffezheim, where Germany's most important races are held every August. Baden-Baden's public is still split equally between addicted gamblers and dedicated health buffs, the former starting their day as the latter bed down for the night.

Baden-Baden naturally attracted César Ritz, who in 1887 took over the Restaurant de la Conversation, which he lit with newly invented electricity concealed among the leaves and branches of tall tropical plants. With its splendid food and music, it quickly became the resort's most fashionable restaurant. For Prince Radziwill, Ritz turned the entire restaurant into a woodland scene, carpeting the floor with turf, lining

Above **A thermal pool at Friedrichsbad was inspired by**

such ancient ruins as the baths of Caracalla. The great

domes and bronze embellished marble Corinthian

columns were intended to bring a classical setting

reminiscent of the grandeur of ancient Rome to the act of

soaking in tepid water.

Schratt, and serenaded by Franz Lehar, who had a house nearby, and Johann Strauss, who adored the cool mountain air. Lehar wrote *The Merry Widow* and many other operettas here, and the genial tenor and *Kammermeister* Richard Tauber learned his roles under the composer's tutelage.

The baths were a cocktail of brine from the salt mines and sulfur from a nearby spring, and the salt concoction was sweetened in late afternoon with *Café und Kuchen* at the Café Walther. Known today as Zauner's, it still serves up sublime pastries, cheesecakes, roulades, and light lunches. The Kurhaus is a modest affair, but the true purpose of visiting spas during the Belle Epoque was fun and social climbing, not health.

the walls with roses, building a goldfish pond, and blanketing the tables with orchids. The elegant hotel, then as now, was Brenner's. The Russian princes, emperors, and kings are gone, but the park is still manicured, the shopping arcade displays the most expensive merchandise of the Via Condotti and Rue de la Paix, and the calèches have been replaced by fleets of Rolls-Royces and Ferraris.

BAD ISCHL

Bad Ischl still bears the imprint of a monarch perhaps even grander than Edward VII. The Hapsburg emperor, Franz Josef I (1830-1916), ruled an empire stretching east from the Austrian border through Hungary and various Balkan powder kegs, and south to Lake Garda in northern Italy. His great palaces in Vienna, the Hofburg and Schloss Schönbrunn, were the centers of a court life of dazzling splendor and stifling protocol. To get away from both, he escaped every summer to Bad Ischl, nestled between the mountains of the Salzkammergut. A man of habit, the emperor spent sixty-six summers of his long reign at the Kaiservilla, a rather modest palace by Hapsburg standards, whose distinguishing feature is the endless rows of horns studding nearly every wall. Until he returned to Vienna—always on August 18—he was visited by nearly every European ruling head of state, and from Ischl he ruled his empire with a steady, loving hand. He was also visited by his beloved mistress, Katharina

The Emperor Franz Josef I (1830–1916) rides in a shooting brake with King George V at Bad Ischl in 1910. The Kaiservilla at Ischl, where the Emperor religiously spent every summer, was the center from which the mighty kaiser ran his vast-flung empire in between shooting anything that moved in the nearby forests. Monarchs and heads of state were regular visitors and rode through the streets of this small and quaint resort to the delight of the cure-takers as well as of the local population. Modest by royal standards of the time, the Biedermeier palace (still the property of Hapsburg descendants) is chock-a-block with hunting trophies which inspired a contemporary—and humane—British ambassador to query when the slaughter would stop.

Above A guest at Karlsbad checks his bill as he leaves his luxury hotel while the staff eagerly wait for their tips. A cure was a fairly long and expensive procedure taken in conditions of substantial comfort. ***Below*** A rich traveler is greeted at the Vittel Palace as he arrives in the hotel's own carriage. Until recently, the railroad stations' platforms were filled with liveried representatives of a resort's grand hotels, who helped guests with their baggage and guided them to their lodgings.

THE
RAILROADS

Lady Waiting on a Station

by James Tissot, 1871–3.

Dunedin Art Gallery, New Zealand.

During the Industrial Revolution new wealth multiplied trade and the doctrine of *laisser faire* broke down national boundaries, creating an increased flow of goods and services and the need for people of many nations to be in closer touch. In Europe, the great bankers—Rothschilds, Barings, Baron de Hirsch, the Anglo-American J.P. Morgan, the Warburgs in Germany and the de Gunzburgs in Russia—saw trade on a world scale. They financed the great railways that knit together the multiple states of the world, and used the rails to transport raw materials, finished products and people.

In America, Abraham Lincoln signed the Pacific Railroad Act on July 1, 1862, forcing the cooperation of the rival Union Pacific and Central Pacific in view of uniting the East and West coasts of the United States along the longest continuous railroad track in the world. Boatloads of Chinamen, coolies with straw hats, were brought over to work for starvation wages—a dollar a day, and there was no insurance against the bows and arrows of furious Indian tribes whose natural paradise and cherished territory was being torn asunder by the pioneer railwaymen. On May 10, 1869, the nation was linked together at Promontory Point, near Utah's Great Salt Lake. There is a famous picture of the workers posing in front of the cow catchers attached onto the locomotives as golden spikes were driven into the penultimate stretch of rail. Meanwhile, in Europe the great bankers fought to replace multiple gauge tracks with a single gauge. Railroads had been considered previously only in terms of national security, and the goal was to prevent different nations from using each other's rails. The bankers slowly succeeded, and then tackled the Alps.

Above East meets West at Promontory Point, linking together the United States on May 10, 1869. Control of railroad lines was split between many companies, controlled by titans of finance, who made vast fortunes in transportation. Bringing the owners together was a feat that needed government intervention, and the building of a cross-country line through the deserts and mountains of the West was an extraordinary accomplishment at the time. *Opposite* Work in progress at a viaduct at Villedomet, in France's Indre-et-Loire region. This viaduct, built by the engineer Salacroup after the war of 1870–71, demonstrates the difficulties involved in bringing railroads through mountainous terrain with the limited technical means available at the end of the last century.

TUNNELS

The only way to economically link north and south was to tunnel through this formidable natural obstacle. The first attempt was the Semmering, the trans-Alpine railway link joining Vienna to Trieste. This was the creation of Carl von Ghéga, a brilliant engineer born in Venice in 1802. Von Ghéga built the Kaiser Ferdinand Nordbahn, the first Austrian railroad between Vienna and Brunn and the personal property of the monarch, and went on to lay down tracks in the Tyrol and Vorarlberg. He was asked to devise a way to get through the Alps without the use of traction at a period when a railroad's slope could not exceed 2° in Europe and 3° in the United States. The Semmering line started north at Glognitz at 437 meters and ended at Munzauschlag at 680 meters. This giant project took four years, a toll of 750 lives and ended in October 1853. The trains had to negotiate 109 steep curves, 16 viaducts and 15 tunnels, the longest being 1,434 meters at an altitude of 898 meters above sea level, the highest level of the line. The young Austrian Emperor Franz Joseph negotiated the pass in an open wagon in the company of von Ghéga on April 12, 1854. Before the Semmering, His Royal and Imperial Highness would have been obliged to leave his train on one side of

the Alps, mount the snowy slopes on the back of a mule and descend on a sled to join another train to continue his trip south.

The construction of the Semmering, in the popular imagination, could be compared to the building of the Channel Tunnel today. The same could be said of the Mount Cenis Tunnel which was to link Savoia to Piedmont. One could travel on the Route Napoleon, but this took 13 hours by diligence and it was closed in winter as its highest point was at 2,000 meters. A customs official from Bardonnèche, M. Medal, proposed drilling a straight line under the Col de Fréjus, 18 kilometers southwest of Mount Cenis, as this was the shortest cut through the formidable Alps. He submitted his project to the King of Piedmont in 1839, and in 1845 His Majesty engaged a Belgian engineer, Henri Maus, to put the plan to work. Maus realized that the key was an efficient method of blasting through rock, but the political climate and war with Austria postponed the great project for a decade. Finally, on September 1, 1857, the first mine was put in place and blasted in the presence of King Vittorio Emmanuel of Savoia. Additional skirmishes with Austria ended with the unification of Italy under Garibaldi and the ceding of Savoia to France in 1859. Suddenly, the construction of the Mount Cenis became a Franco-Italian project, with each nation quibbling about money. The French thought the whole enterprise was folly and paid far less than the more optimistic Italians. One team started drilling at Modane, at a height of 1,057 meters, the other in Bardonnèche at 1,260 meters, the idea being to shake hands at six kilometers from each end at a height of 1,298 meters. Work proceeded at a snail's pace, the blasting machines broke down, the miserable workers were reduced to pickaxes, and were at tremendous risk from falling rock and freezing underground streams. Finally, in January 1861, pneumatic drills were put into service on the Italian side and a year later on the French side. At last, the job could proceed at full speed (in 1860s terms!).

On Christmas Day 1870, two wet and dirty teams of human moles finally got together as the last wall of rock separating them was blasted away, thirty-one years after the tunnel's conception. There are no

The first locomotive goes through the Mount Cenis Tunnel on September 17, 1871, linking France to Italy through the Col de Fréjus. From conception to completion, the tunnel took thirty-one years and was the inspiration for similar projects which linked Europe by permitting year-round passage through its formidable mountain barriers. Transport of freight and passengers increased dramatically, and long-distance trips in luxury trains were but one of the radical changes in the history of travel made possible by these Herculean engineering feats. Originally, passengers feared asphyxiation from the trains' exhaust, not to mention floods and falling rock. All the great tunnels built at the end of the century still function perfectly.

details concerning the workers' Christmas dinner, but on September 17, 1871, French and Italian officials celebrated the tunnel's opening with a twenty-course feast from soup to nuts, going through hors d'oeuvres, roasts, game, and several desserts.

There was a good deal of apprehension as the portly bureaucrats entered the long, dark tunnel at exactly 10:40 A.M. A journalist reported, "We had heard so often how dangerous the trip would be, how the heat and smoke would be intolerable, that we were seized by a gnawing anxiety despite ourselves. During the crossing, I lowered the foggy window and was astonished as cold and fresh air hit my face. Nearly no smoke, a temperature of 23 or 24 degrees. At 11:23, exactly 43 minutes after entering the tunnel, we got out of the immense hole and arrived at Bardonnèche."

Freight and passengers could now go through so easily that travel and commerce were transformed. The Mount Cenis Tunnel was followed by the Saint Gotthard, linking Germany to Italy through Switzerland. The Gotthard, like other tunnels, cost a fortune, and nearly two hundred men's lives were lost during its construction. Its main backer, Louis Favre, died of a heart attack on the job site in 1879. The direct line from Lucerne to Chiasso was built in 1882. During its first year of service, a million people and 455,000 tons

A viaduct at Giornica on the Saint Gotthard line linking Germany to Italy via Switzerland. Finished in 1882, this line crosses 520 bridges and viaducts, passes through 71 tunnels, and traverses some of the most beautiful scenery in Europe.

of merchandise poured through the tunnel; ten years later, those figures had more than doubled, and they have increased constantly ever since.

Later engineers learned from the pioneering efforts of von Ghéga on the Semmering, Henri Maus and Germain Sommeiller on the Mount Cenis, and Louis Favre on the Saint Gotthard. They built other tunnels more efficiently. The 10,250-meter Arlberg Tunnel of 1883 linked Vienna to the Swiss frontier; the Giovi Tunnel forged the missing link on the much-traveled Milan–Genoa line. The twenty-kilometer Simplon Tunnel became the longest railroad tunnel in the world and gave its name to the famous train that passed through it from Paris to Istanbul—the Simplon Orient Express. Nine other railroad tunnels were built in this century, which also saw the construction of spectacular mountain routes and tunnels for automobile travel.

GEORGE PULLMAN

The rapid development of railroads finally permitted uninterrupted long-distance travel—and ended long nights of sitting upright in rows on hard seats as trains crossed the great expanses of the United States or

Europe. Luxury travel had to make tracks, and nobody understood that better than George Mortimer Pullman in Chicago and Georges Nagelmackers in Belgium.

The word Pullman has become part of our vocabulary. In the United States, it still brings to mind individual compartments on a luxury train. In Europe, alas, it now evokes the vision of crowded tourist buses, thanks to mass-travel promoters who have misapplied the glory of the name to cramped, air-conditioned people-conveyors. There was a time, however, when true Pullman cars were attached to the great trains of the United States, Great Britain, Europe, and even China and Egypt.

George Mortimer Pullman has been described as 1% inventor, 9% improver and 90% businessman. He typified a new generation of self-made men who revelled in their simple origins and achievements. He was born in Brockton, New York, on March 3, 1831, the third of ten children. He and his brother Albert were very close. Albert was a gifted carpenter and in 1848 George traveled around the United States selling the cabinets and other furniture manufactured by his brother. It is probable that the feeling for cabinetry inspired George when he built his great carriages.

In 1853 he sat up all night on the short trip from Buffalo to Westfield. The train lurched violently, the passengers emerged covered with soot and exhausted after

Above **A drawing of the Colonist's sleeping car on the Canadian Pacific Railway seems to represent day and night simultaneously in order to demonstrate both sleeping and sitting accommodations at the time.** *Below* **A CIWL car in service between 1905 and 1915 on the Paris-Deauville-Trouville Express.** *Inset* **George Pullman (1831–1897), whose comfortable sleeping cars radically changed the concept of long-distance travel.** *Opposite* **A mother combs the hair of her child in 1905 on one of the three Pullman sleeping cars in the Santa Fe Railroad's California Limited.**

immobile hours on uncomfortable benches. There was no heating, one was lucky to find a candle to read by, sanitary facilities were non-existent and food was either taken in a basket or grabbed from a station buffet. Nothing better describes the conditions than the satirist Daumier's masterpiece "Le Wagon du Troisième Classe" where an odd assortment of cramped people are bathed in a brownish gloom. Pullman quickly decided that sitting up all night in trains had to come to an end, and that peddling Albert's furniture had no future. He moved to Chicago, a booming town, and specialized in moving entire buildings from one site to the other. One of his great feats was moving the four-storey Tremont House without breaking a window. As a publicity stunt, he transported the structure with guests and servants inside as astonished bystanders watched the moving hotel.

His next feat was to borrow two coaches from a local railroad and refurbish them. He installed wood paneling, plush chairs, and, perhaps inspired by Albert's cabinetry, fitted seats that folded down into beds. The two cars ran between Chicago and Bloomington for a fare supplement of fifty cents a head, and they had their own porter, Jonathan L. Barnes, to care for the passengers, make up beds, and distribute

oil lamps. Barnes, a white man, was the precursor of several generations of black porters who spent their lives crossing the country polishing shoes, serving drinks at all hours, handling baggage, and making up berths. He was also the ancestor of the Wagons-Lits attendant who crossed Europe with a briefcase full of passports and customs declarations, dealing with tiresome officials in several languages while his passengers slept happily between crisp linen sheets.

The Civil War put a temporary stop to Pullman's business since the Unionists confiscated all rolling stock for their epic struggle. Pullman was no hero and promptly went West to make a fortune selling equipment, food and other necessities at Gregory Gulch in Colorado to prospectors whose gold nuggets were burning holes in their pockets. At the end of the conflict, Pullman went back to Chicago and invested his entire fortune of $20,000—an enormous sum at the time—into building the most luxurious, extravagant and useless wagon yet intended to travel by rail. Its walnut interiors, framed mirrors, extensive use of polished brass and deep pile carpeting set the tone for Pullman's later carriages. "Pioneer" was a white elephant, mounted on bogies with four axles instead of two, and was so wide and high that it couldn't travel without hitting bridges, platforms and other obstacles in its way. To absorb the inevitable friction and noise between wheel and track, Pioneer was so heavily reinforced that when its 27 tons were placed on the tracks it couldn't move: it was pushed into a shed and quickly renamed "Pullman's Folly".

On April 15, 1865, Abraham Lincoln was assassinated by John Wilkes Booth. The president's body was to be shipped aboard a special train from Washington to Springfield, Illinois, Lincoln's birthplace. Arrangements for the run between Chicago and Springfield were to be made by Colonel James Bowen, president of the bank in which Pullman had his account. Pullman saw his great opportunity clearly and convinced Bowen that the great man's remains must travel their last mile in the world's most luxurious carriage. The Pioneer was wheeled out and quickly adapted, while the railroaders worked night and day trimming anything that the huge car might smash into. Thousands lined the tracks on May 2, 1865, as the Pioneer

Above The bridal suite in the Pullman car "Republic," used in the Pennsylvania Railroad's famous "Broadway Limited" around 1900 between New York and Chicago. *Opposite* The observation car on "Golden Gage," one of Pullman's private cars built in 1889. These sumptuous carriages were the status symbols of the super rich until World War II. The equivalent of today's corporate jet, they were built to the owners' specifications and their manufacture was a highly profitable activity for the Pullman Company. Among the main clients for the private cars, or "varnish," were the owners of America's railroads.

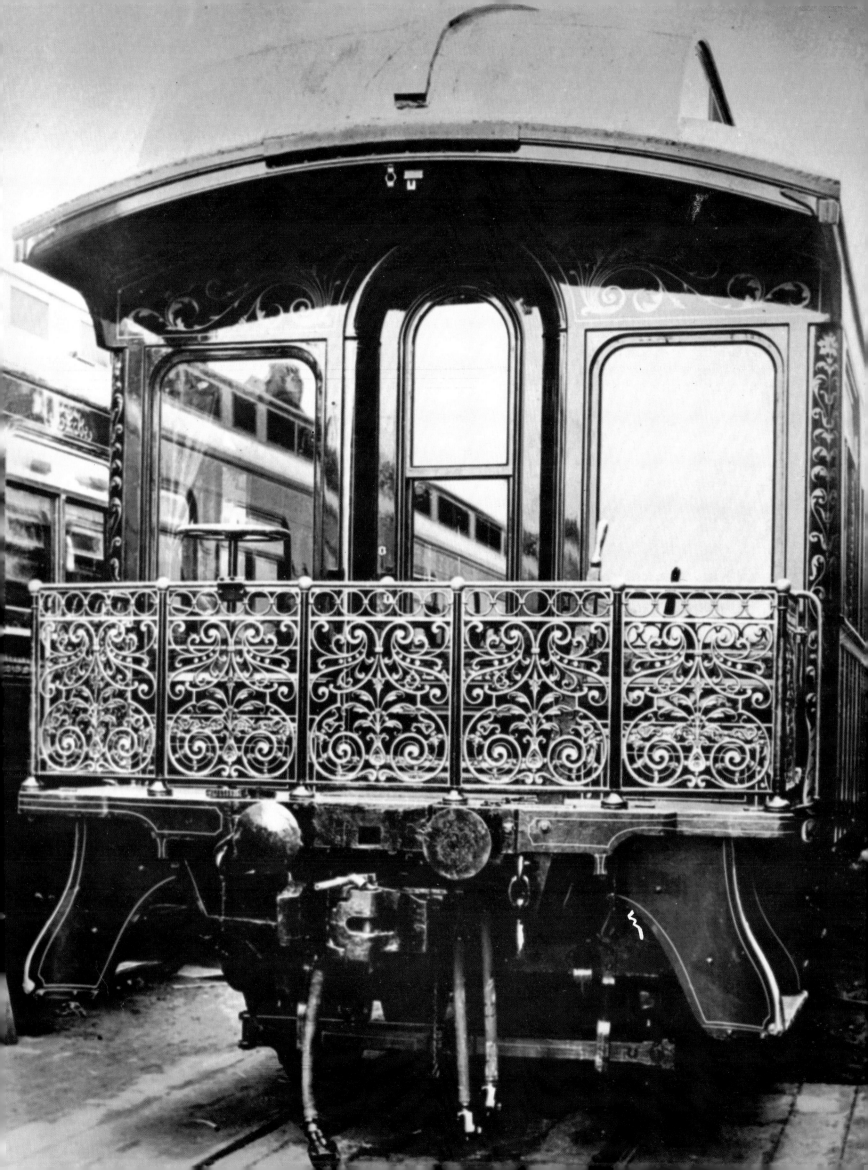

passed; the national tabloids published drawings of its interiors, and Pullman was instantly launched as a titan of the rails. Pullman also offered the Pioneer to General Ulysses S. Grant when he was elected president four years later, and so the Michigan Central Railroad was obliged to perform the alterations necessary to protect its property from the luxury monster.

Other entrepreneurs also built sleeping cars at the time, but Pullman had the competitive edge: he was the supplier of presidents; it hardly mattered whether they were alive or dead.

In 1867, with forty-eight cars in service, he created the Pullman Company. Its subsidiaries included the Pullman Standard Car Company, which manufactured the carriages, and the Pullman Palace Car Company, Inc., which operated them. That year saw the introduction of the first dining car, named Delmonico after the famous restaurant in New York City. Its menu was somewhat limited, but dining cars rapidly became social centers on the many trains crossing the country. Pullman's sleeping accommodations were somewhat racy: beds were lined up in two tiers, hidden from the corridor by a heavy curtain. Ladies and gents slept head-to-foot in an age when women had separate sitting and dining rooms in America's new grand hotels. There was a whiff of impropriety until separate compartments were built, but some of those old, cheerfully indiscreet carriages still plied the less-

traveled routes of the United States until the 1960s.

The demand for his cars obliged Pullman to build a huge factory at Lake Calumet, fourteen miles south of Chicago. It became the center of America's first planned industrial city, completed in 1881. The city was named for him, and Pullman rapidly assumed a dictatorial attitude. He attempted to control all aspects of his employees' work and lives, and called in the police to settle any disagreements between management and labor.

GEORGES NAGELMACKERS

In 1868 a young Belgian banker named Georges Nagelmackers arrived in the United States. This scion of a distinguished European family could not have been more different from the huckster Pullman. His father, a friend of King Leopold II, was a rich banker, and there was no need for young Georges to make a living. But he and Pullman had one thing in common: they were both fascinated by the potential of improving passenger travel by rail in an age when the big money was made on freight. Young Georges had already thought of ways to extend railway travel across national borders, but he lost his head to an older woman. He sunk into a depression, and his parents decided to send him off to America to recover.

The United States, then as now, captivated the young with its energy and opportunities. The

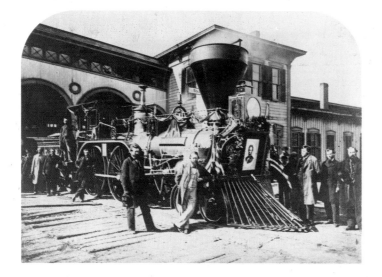

Above A contemporary engraving of the Frank Leslie excursion from Chicago to the Pacific in a Pullman car in 1877. The berths, protected by only a curtain, were looked upon as somewhat licentious at the time; flirtation was clearly not an issue on this particular trip. *Below* The engine used to pull President Lincoln's funeral train in 1865. One of the cars used was Pullman's "Pioneer," as only the best would serve for the last trip of the beloved leader. *Opposite* Passengers embark on Pullman cars in 1905. The concertina vestibule sprang one car against the next, assuring greater stability than a central coupling and open gangway between two open platforms. It allowed passengers to move more easily between cars and keep dry in rainy weather.

Nagelmackers name opened doors, and young Georges headed for the offices of the leading railroads. He quickly learned about such things as wheel design, compensating for poor trackage with better carriage design, and the new Westinghouse compressed-air braking system, but, most important, he arranged to meet Pullman and ride on his famous Pioneer. The unsuspecting Pullman showed the young Belgian his workshop and explained his railroad contracts, unwittingly giving away trade secrets to the man who would become his great competitor. Back home, Georges published a paper entitled *Projet de l'installation de wagons-lits sur les chemins de fer du continent*, published in 1870. Had his parents sent him to Russia he might have traveled from Kiev to Odessa in a carriage with reclining armchairs and a bathroom, but czarist Russia trailed the United States in luxury train travel. Nagelmackers wrote:

> Which tourist or businessman traveling, for example, between Berlin and Cologne or Paris and Marseilles, would not happily enter a car in which, for an entire night he could stretch out onto a bed made up with sheets and blanket, delivering himself—without fear of being disturbed—to sweet sleep, waking up in the morning a few kilometers from his destination.

His project was highly developed. Plates illustrated three types of carriages, one with separate compartments accessed by a corridor. From Pullman, he stole the idea of folding beds and porters, and foresaw individual compartments, called *chambrettes* reserved for ladies; in the plan there were also compartments for two or more people. Most important, he set out that this service was not to be supplied by railway companies but by a totally separate entity which would supply the cars and servants to different lines on a contractual basis. He would make his profit by charging a luxury supplement for each passenger and getting paid for meals, drinks and any extra services, while the railroad would collect its regular first class fare. So complete was the plan that it only lacked a color plate of a steel carriage, painted deep blue,

Above George Nagelmackers, the legendary founder of CIWL, photographed in Brussels on January 4, 1898 at the height of his career. The empire he founded in 1872 is still flourishing today. *Opposite* Interiors of cars on the Odessa-Kiev line in 1864. Imperial Russia had a high standard of comfort on its trains before the great Nagelmackers founded his enterprise, and these were the first of many comfortable sleeping and dining cars to cross the Russian empire.

INTÉRIEUR DU WAGON·RESTAURANT

CUISINE DU WAGON·RESTAURANT

COUPÉ D'UNE VOITURE DE 2ᵐᵉ CLASSE

CABINET DE TOILETTE DE 2ᵐᵉ CLASSE

COUPÉ DE 1ʳᵉ CLASSE, DE JOUR

COUPÉ DE 1ʳᵉ CLASSE, DE NUIT

embellished with arms bearing the WL logo, proudly franked with brown liveried servants wearing the Wagon Lits kepi.

At the age of 25, Nagelmackers sent his treatise to several railway companies and banks who were sufficiently impressed to let him attempt to convert theory to reality on the Paris-Vienna line. Sadly, less than a month later, on July 15, 1870, the Franco-Prussian War was declared, sinking the project. At the end of the hostilities, in 1871, Nagelmackers's father got the ear of the Belgian King Leopold II (one of the true gilded and pleasure-loving travelers), and His Majesty

in 1872 granted a concession to the young entrepreneur to run a car on the Ostend-Brindisi route used by the Indian Mail which was the link between Britain and the jewel in the crown of its Empire.

The King, a shrewd businessman, also agreed to head a list of potential capital subscribers, making it far easier for young Nagelmackers to raise the money he needed. In modern parlance, he wrote himself a stock option, and in time the CIWL stock became one of his best investments (admittedly dwarfed by the King's vast holdings in the Belgian Congo.) That summer, Nagelmackers got back the Paris-Vienna concession that

Queen Marie of Romania is greeted at Belgrade Station in 1923 after

descending from her private carriage at the conclusion of a trip to Paris.

The queen of this oil-rich country built several palaces in beautiful sites.

Proust had remarked on her small and proud head, and in her jewel case

were the largest sapphire in the world and the most beautiful necklace of

pearls ever strung together.

now went through the new Semmering line and in October he founded the renowned "Compagnie Internationale des Wagons Lits" with five four-wheel cars built in Semmering at a cost of 20,000 francs each. The new company was an immediate success and was treated in Europe as a revolution in travel. The sleeping car had magically vaporized borders for those fortunate enough to be able to pay the supplement, and the first "European Timetables Conference" was called to regulate international travel. Perhaps the scale of the venture was too large, Nagelmackers too bold or too visionary. Once the great adventure had started and real money was needed, the banks pulled the rug from under the entrepreneur's feet.

COLONEL WILLIAM MANN

Fortunately, an American adventurer and speculator, Colonel William d'Alton Mann, had heard of Nagelmackers and invited him to London, where he was living in great style on the somewhat shady profits from his oil explorations in Pennsylvania, tax collecting in Alabama, and equipment sales during the Civil War. Mann, who always seemed to be just a step ahead of the law, had also dabbled in luxury railway cars, even building one for the famous Lillie Langtry. Despite the solid-silver bathroom fixtures, a bedroom padded in Lyons silk, and a modern kitchen, Mann claimed the actress's car was a replica of Cleopatra's barge.

But Mann was unable to break Pullman's grip on the new industry even though he had very original plans for carriages with boudoirs, living rooms and bathrooms much along the lines laid out by Nagelmackers. He sailed for England, founded the Mann Boudoir Sleeping Company, and opened a Pullman-like factory in Lancashire. Mann and Nagelmackers were on the same wavelength, and Mann's well-financed company absorbed Nagelmackers's capital-starved enterprise. CIWL disappeared for the moment to become Mann's Railway Carriage Company Ltd. Nagelmackers's

King Leopold of Belgium descends from his CIWL car onto a special carpet at Beaulieu station

in the south of France in 1908. Known as "Le Roi Cleopolde" because of his liaison with the

courtesan Cleo de Merode, King Leopold built her a splendid villa in Beaulieu overlooking the

Mediterranean, where he could behave with more abandon than was possible in his staid

capital. Fabulously rich from investments in the Belgian Congo (now Zaire), King Leopold was

one of the first backers of CIWL's founder Georges Nagelmackers.

AGONS-LITS et des GRANDS EXPRESS

Cⁱᵉ INTERNATIONALE
DES WAGONS-LITS
ET DES
GRANDS EXPRESS

Légende

Trains de luxe
Wagons-Lits
Wagons-Restᵗˢ
Hôtels
Hôtels correspondants ᴀ
Agences de la Cⁱᵉ Intˡˢ
des Wagons-Lits
et Bureaux de Vente

Extrême-Orient

Imprimerie Centrale de la Bourse, ALCAN LÉVY, 117, Rue Réaumur, PARIS

concessions combined with Mann's carriages and money resulted in a fabulous merger, although the entrepreneurs' personalities were very different (there is only one known photograph of them together). The company quickly turned a profit, and Mann pulled a Pullman by providing one of his cars for the Prince of Wales's trip to Saint Petersburg for the marriage of his brother Alfred, the Duke of Edinburgh, to Princess Marie Romanov, the daughter of Czar Alexander II.

RIVALS IN EUROPE

It was too good to last. In 1873 Pullman was brought over to England by Sir James Allport of the powerful Midland Railway. The result was an all-out battle. Pullman made forays into Italy and France but was dominant only in Britain. Nagelmackers and a group of financiers bought out Mann for $5,000,000 and he returned to New York. King Leopold led a new capital subscription and a revived CIWL dominated Europe, later reaching the Russian steppes, Manchuria, and China. In 1908, Lord Dalziel bought the assets of the British Pullman, and his daughter married Nagelmackers's son René, bringing the CIWL and Pullman into an incestuous relationship. Meanwhile, ministers were

bribed, kings seduced, and bankers bamboozled. Speculators became rich on railway shares and bonds, while the effort to open new lines, build better cars, and improve service created the most splendid and opulent way of life ever enjoyed on rails.

VARNISH

In Europe, private trains were largely the preserve of heads of state and royals, while in the New World they were the essential status symbol of the parvenu. Nobody of means ever traveled with ordinary passengers;

Above left Georges Nagelmackers (standing), founder of CIWL, and his one time partner, the slightly dubious American promoter William d'Alton Mann (seated). They are posing in 1873 in front of one of Colonel Mann's early boudoir sleeping cars. *Above right* Thirty-seven years later, in 1910, Italy's Crown Prince Umberto—the last of the few members of the Savoia family to reign over a united Italy—steps down from a CIWL carriage at Milan Station on the occasion of a visit to the 1910 Universal Exhibition. *Inset* The Wagons Lits insignia.

they either owned or rented their own cars, or were guests on somebody else's. Mrs. Edward T. Stotesbury, one of the doyennes of New York and Palm Beach society, once told a reporter that "the only thing that's economical about our car is the solid-gold plumbing. It saves polishing, you know." She was probably right, since the possession of private rolling stock (known as "varnish," after the highly polished cabinetry) by the elite of the United States involved a special staff of servants, monogrammed gold plate, personal mechanics, and at least two French chefs.

It was George Pullman who filled most of the orders, since he had established a reputation as the leading purveyor of luxury cars to the great railroad companies of the land. His main competition was the Vanderbilt-controlled Wagner Palace Car Company, until the rivals merged in 1899. Other coach builders included Colonel William d'Alton Mann (who as George Nagelmackers's partner had played a pivotal role in the development of the CIWL), Barney and Smith, American Car and Foundry, and, on the West Coast, the Union and Risden Iron Works. The first private car was built for President Lincoln by the U.S. Military Authority during the Civil War, and it joined Pullman's Pioneer on the

Afternoon tea in the Pullman, around 1926, on the "Flèche d'Or" between Calais and

Paris. "The Golden Arrow," its counterpart, took passengers from London to Dover.

This wonderful service ran for several years after the end of World War II, and the

ration of space to passenger, the impeccable service and food, and the warmth and

elegance of the Art Deco decoration made the voyage an absolute delight unless a rough

Channel crossing spoiled the day.

president's funeral cortege. Until the 1960s, in fact, presidential candidates conducted nationwide ''whistle-stop campaigns'' in private trains, exhorting the electorate from the brass-railed observation platform at the rear of the train. This canopied overhang, a characteristic appurtenance of the private railway car, was used as a veranda from which to view the passing countryside.

Life on the rails, for the magnificoes of the United States, was really an extension of Fifth Avenue or Nob Hill. To private citizens who started buying their cars at the end of the Civil War on the wave of prosperity engendered by reconstruction, there were two essential appurtenances: a wall safe and an English butler. The safe, needless to say, contained the jewels needed by the lady of the car when she and her guests dressed for dinner, the gentlemen in white tie, the ladies in the latest evening gowns from Worth and, later, Poiret. The host's servants were dressed in house livery, cupboards were filled with gold plate especially made for

the car and engraved with its name, French chefs prepared magnificent meals, and the stiffly anonymous British butler made sure that the entire procedure strictly followed the rites of the aristocracy that his newly rich American employers apishly followed. Some could afford only one car, whose price escalated from $50,000 after the Civil War to over $500,000 between the two world wars. It contained a bathroom (with a generous curled-ledge tub to keep water from splashing out as the train lurched); a small kitchen; a living room wainscoted in Pullman's mahogany; plush seats and a table on which up to eight could dine; a few bedrooms with comfortable brass beds; and gaslight, later replaced with electricity. Earlier cars had the Pullman folding beds on the floor and tuck-away beds hidden in the mahogany paneling above, all curtained off at night. Design was dictated by the whims of the client. Some set aside an area for working at a desk, others devoted more space to dining or sleeping,

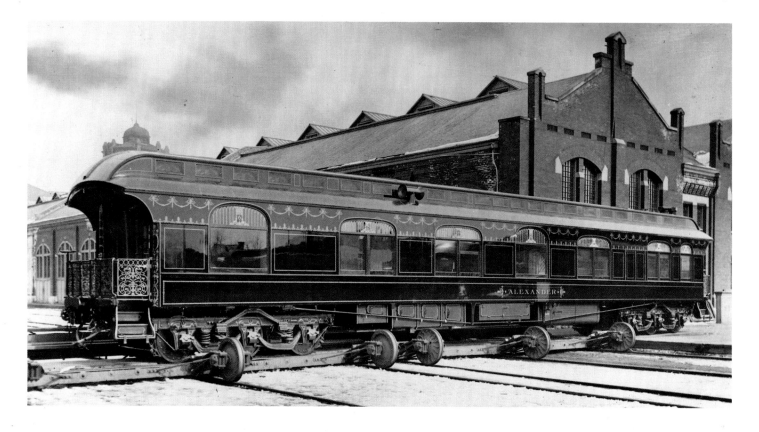

Above **The beautiful private varnish ''Alexander'' built in 1890 by the Pullman Palace Car Co. for A.A. McLeod, President of the Philadelphia and Reading Railroad. The transport magnates extended to each other the courtesy of their tracks, and regularly lent their ''varnish'' to friends and business relations.** *Opposite* **One of several cars that were built by Pullman in 1898 for the private train of Mexico's dictator, Porfirio Diaz. This presidential train was perhaps the most luxurious ever produced and was in every detail as plush and opulent as the great new palace hotels of Europe. At the time, Mexico enjoyed immense wealth from its mines, much of which flowed into the pockets of its chief of state.**

and one lascivious owner could press a button that made one bedroom wall instantly disappear, thus revealing his surprised neighbor.

A private car (or suite of cars) was always fitted onto the back of the train to avoid the unthinkable catastrophe of being crossed by ordinary passengers looking for friends in other parts of the train. Nevertheless, the owners did have to put up with an occasional visit from the train's engineer. Private cars were linked to great expresses and even commuter trains. For this privilege, the owner was charged a fee by the railroads that owned the lines on which he was riding. In fact, many of the cars traveled free since the great majority belonged either to owners of the great railways or their bankers, who were in the habit of lending their cars to friends, business associates, and family. Most of the great fortunes between the Civil War and World War I were made in transportation, and this particular segment of society's robber barons extended to each other the courtesy of its tracks.

The Goulds, Vanderbilts, Goelets, and Stanfords had suites of several cars pulled by a special engine, which avoided the discomfort of the cars' stopping where ordinary mortals got off. A private train generally consisted of a large car directly behind the engine for luggage, fresh provisions, wines, and champagne; a car with sleeping accommodations for servants; a dining car with full kitchen, pantry, and several tables; several sleeping cars with full or convertible beds; and a saloon car with its observation platform. Various owners added cars for special needs. Pullman himself used one for his horses, carriages, grooms, and coachmen, while the dyspeptic Jay Gould took along his own cow, whose butterfat content agreed with his delicate stomach. Decoration followed the owner's fancy, and ranged from the Gothic cathedral to the Empire splendor of Malmaison. Particular emphasis was placed on fin-de-siècle patterned carpets, tasseled damask curtains, tufted velvet sofas, shining mahogany columns, and vaulted frescoed ceilings. J. P. Morgan never owned a train, but, in atonement for his sins, once chartered from Pullman a long series of cars—including a domed barber shop—to transport a group of Episcopalian bishops to a meeting in San Francisco.

Special stops for tycoons on regular trains posed no problems. Otto Kahn's private varnish was attached every evening to a train of ordinary commuters from the canyons of Wall Street, and the train always stopped on a special siding so that the nattily dressed, mustachioed tycoon could descend with his guests to a waiting fleet of cars; the train would pick everybody up the next morning. Time was not of the essence if a great banker was being pulled by a train filled with people eager to join their families after a hot and busy day in the city. Incidentally, Kahn's colleagues who lived on Long Island Sound generally made their way to work on board their great transatlantic steam yachts, which moored at the New York Yacht Club's pier downtown. This was a magical time when the rich went to work in super-luxe style, were served coffee and cigars by their valets, and relaxed on the way home with drinks while they finished up their business.

You did not need to own your own car to travel in privacy. Until 1941, Pullman kept a fleet available for charter, moving the cars around the country according to the season. This meant Florida in the winter, Maine and Saratoga in the summer, and the great cities the rest of the year. In the early days of this service the cost was fifty dollars a day plus a first-class fare for each passenger, but chartering a car had no cachet; it was like renting somebody's summerhouse. A successful man owned his varnish, filled it all year with servants, and felt no qualms about using it a few weeks a year. It was "in season" that the private cars flocked like migrating birds to the northern or southern Atlantic shores.

Opposite **Charles M. Schub's "Loretto", built by Pullman in 1901. The mahogany-**

paneled stateroom, with its double-bed covered in embroidered lace, is quite typical of

the standard of comfort enjoyed on private cars at the turn of the century. *Above*

Royalty traveled in great style on the rails as can be seen in Victoria's day saloon, one of

several cars making up her train.

Everybody traveled to Florida in their own varnish, to Flagler's Hotel del Coronado in Saint Augustine or the Royal Poinciana in Palm Beach. The hotels had special sidings for the cars, and private servants stayed aboard while the owners took over great suites in the palm-filled hotels. People did not think of their lackeys' discomfort as the hot Florida sun turned the immobile cars into ovens. The first air-conditioning was produced for the yeast-rich Fleischmanns' Edgewood in the 1930s. Around the same time, the beer-rich Budweisers installed in the Adolphus's guest rooms taps from which their ice-chilled beverage flowed in an endless stream. It is unknown whether this amenity was available to those who assured their comfort, but we must assume that a beer-filled butler or maid would not have been well taken. Sidings for private cars were very much part of the travel scene until World War II. They exist unused today underneath the main entrance to New York City's Waldorf-Astoria on Park Avenue and Fiftieth Street. When the hotel opened in 1932, in the depths of the Great Depression, the Waldorf's sidings were totally filled and many private cars had to be parked in Grand Central Station.

TRAVELING ENTERTAINERS
Railroad tycoons and bankers, as well as rich industrialists, were not the only owners of their own private

varnish. Successful artists—actors, pianists, and particularly opera singers—traveled throughout the United States in their own cars, thus avoiding the discomfort and loneliness of hotels in provincial cities. After the disappearance of private cars, one of the major complaints of great musicians was the impossibility of finding even a crust of bread after a performance. Lillie Langtry, on the other hand, in her City of Worcester, ordered up a late supper of broiled quails, tenderloin steak, French peas, potatoes, cheese, coffee, bananas, and grapes, all perfectly cooked by her French chef Méziar and served by her English butler Beverly. Another obvious problem for musicians was practicing or vocalizing, noise to which other hotel guests furiously objected. Paderewski obviously had a grand piano in the living room of his car, the General Stanley, and Adelina Patti could run up and down her scales to her heart's delight.

She had a car named after her which was produced by the Mann Boudoir-Car Company. A reporter from the "Call" described it as follows:

The hammered gold and silver effect of the sides and ceiling was in a design of morning glories. The parlor was lighted by plate glass windows and a gold lamp which hung from above. The windows were ornamented with designs representing the four seasons. The hand-carved piano of natural wood corresponded with the rest of the woodwork in the room. There was a couch with satin pillows ornamented with bows and lace tidies opposite the piano. A square table covered with plush, stood in the center and all around were easy chairs of luxurious depth. Mme. Patti's bedroom was largely pink. The paneling was of satinwood, inlaid with ebony, gold and amaranth. Bevelled mirrors were abundant and the couch had a silk-plush cover of gold embroidered with trailing pink rosebuds and with the monogram "A.P." in the same delicate shade. Over the velvet carpet, beside the bed, was a leopard skin. A stand was mounted with silver and a small bathtub was concealed from view by mirrored doors. There was a closet containing the table service of solid silver, china and glass—all with the diva's monogram.

Inset A retouched, and flattering, photograph of the dreaded tycoon J.P. Morgan, one of the pillars of world finance. *Above* Edward VII commissioned a new train to travel throughout Great Britain. The bedrooms, with cozy curtains and a brass bed covered with a quilted satin bed spread, communicated with the monarch's dressing room. *Opposite and overleaf* The bathroom and kitchen of the Viceregal train used in 1904–1905.

The last remnant of traveling troupers is the Ringling Brothers Barnum and Bailey circus train, which carries everything from lions to sword swallowers. But circus performers are a far cry from the bigger-than-life artists who once boomed along the tracks to a public clamoring for their talents.

Curiously, owners were very discreet about their private lives on the rails. Pullman's order book was kept under the greatest secrecy, reporters were seldom invited aboard, and shades were kept drawn while the trains waited in the station. Tycoons were also exceedingly fussy about selling used cars, and often preferred to have them destroyed. Alas, only a few remain in railway museums across the United States.

The Russian royals—as always—had the grandest train, a long suite of dark-blue wooden carriages bearing the double-headed eagle, and the state ran three identical trains along the tracks to confuse terrorists who were always out to blow up the Imperial Family on their way to their estates in Poland and the Crimea. It was on the Imperial train that Nicholas II learned of the Soviet Revolution, and he returned to Saint Petersburg a prisoner of the new government. One of the last and most remarkable private trains was that of the British Viceroy in India, a suite of carriages nearly as grand as that of the King Emperor himself. It was the only white train allowed on the subcontinent and carried the Viceroy and his court on visits to India's Maharajas. Despite the sun-reflecting qualities of the glistening exterior, the carriages became so hot as the

The kitchen on

the Viceregal Indian train.

monsoon approached that the cold water taps scalded the passengers' hands and even the linen sheets became too hot to lie on. Notwithstanding, the Viceroy always managed to step out on the canopied platform cool as a cucumber, in his white ceremonial uniform and plumes.

The best idea of the luxury of the private car can be obtained by visiting Britain's National Railway Museum at York, where several cars of Britain's monarchs and grandees are perfectly preserved.

THE RAILROAD STATION AND THE GRAND HOTEL

After the skyscraper, the railway station and the grand hotel were the principal architectural innovations of the second half of the nineteenth century. It was in the railway station that steam—the driving force of the Industrial Revolution—most asserted its physical presence. Time ruled these stations; large clocks rose in their towers, were embedded in their stone facades, and were hung on every platform. In many ways, the railway station symbolizes the tragedy of modern times. It saw in the hordes of poor peasants hoping for better lives in the factories and sweatshops of the cities and saw out the desperate emigrants leaving for distant shores. On its concrete platforms, parents were separated from children, lovers parted, soldiers left for war. Billions of hours were wasted in waiting rooms, enough so that children were actually born in stations. Many more souls, however, *left* this world via the Cemetery Station at Waterloo, run by the London Necropolis Company.

But the station could be the start of an exciting adventure or a wonderful vacation. To the gilded traveler, it offered escape on luxury trains, not to mention comfortable first-class waiting rooms and splendid meals in the *buffet de la gare*.

The railway station consists of two parts: the station building itself and the train shed. In 1850, when the first large railway stations were erected, the station building reflected the past. The Baths of Caracalla and the Gothic cathedral were just a few of the eclectic themes applied to stations to convey the important role of transportation in the industrial era. The train sheds embodied the future. Essentially functional, they sheltered passengers against the elements as they boarded or left the trains. Their great ribs of iron were covered in glass, bathing the platforms in a suffused glow of

Above A private railroad siding in the tent city belonging to the Hotel del Coronado off San Diego. This

fashionable resort was the West Coast's answer to the great hotels put up by Henry Flagler in Saint Augustine

and Palm Beach. Tycoons arrived in their private "varnish" to enjoy the season of amusements including

rodeo, concerts and parades. *Below* The summer carriage of the Viceroy of Egypt, which transported him

along the country's newly built tracks. Ottoman influence is evident in the design, and the plethora of

windows cooled the carriage in the heat of the desert.

light. The magnificent vaulted roofs of these sheds are to the industrial age what the soaring Gothic cathedral was to the Middle Ages. Once the airplane and automobile dominated travel, many stations—particularly in the United States—were neglected or abandoned. Today, at least a few have been rediscovered, declared architectural monuments, and even converted into magnificent museums.

The first great stations were built in Great Britain, where the train was born. Paddington Station established the model. It was the creation of Isambard Kingdom Brunel and Matthew Digby Wyatt. Brunel was a remarkably gifted engineer, a famous bridge builder and a visionary. Paddington Station opened in 1851, deliberately coinciding with the Universal Exhibition on view in the Crystal Palace in Hyde Park. Wyatt integrated a hotel into the station, which combined the architecture of ancient Rome with contemporary comfort. Paddington's size reflected the ambitions of this optimistic age: it was built on a heroic scale, and its shed was one of the wonders of its time. Twenty years later came St. Pancras Station, which was even more astonishing. The engineers threw up steel flying buttresses from Gothic walls, and made one of the largest and most beautiful glass cages in the world.

Before the turn of the century, stations were built on the Paddington–St. Pancras model in many great cities. The finest were in Berlin, Frankfurt, Paris, Budapest, Antwerp, and Milan. Travelers stepped out of their trains and into the heart of the city, and their first need was often to find a place to sleep.

THE GRAND HOTEL IN THE UNITED STATES

The earliest hotels, contrary to public opinion, were in the United States, whose democratic character encouraged a full and open society. Up until the 1850s, the privileged few in Europe interacted in palaces, large city houses and country estates. People traveled of necessity and exchanged visits, while the rich and powerful were largely inaccessible and discreet. In the United States, the newly rich wanted to show off, to flaunt their wealth, to boast of their success. Also, the lack of national boundaries encouraged the free movement of people over great distances, and they needed somewhere to stay. That dictated large, comfortable hotels, and eventually encouraged the construction of residential hotels, which were a novelty to Europe until the twentieth century.

The first American hotel was New York's City Hotel of 1794–96. Despite seventy-three rooms on five floors, it was little more than an expanded inn, with little space set aside for public rooms. Isaiah Rogers' Tremont House in Boston was the first luxury hotel in the world. With 170 bedrooms and a dining room capable of seating two hundred—with French chefs and a separate area for ladies—it created considerable excitement when it opened in 1829. It had a splendid domed lobby, mosaic floors, a reading room with foreign newspapers, and a bar of which Charles Dickens wrote that "the stranger is initiated into the mysteries of the gin sling, sherry cobbler, mint julep, zangree, timber doodle and other rare drinks." Highly unusual for its time were the individual rooms with locks, a proper bed, rugs, curtains, and maids who brought water pitchers and a valuable piece of soap. William Eliot's monograph, *A Description of Tremont House, with Architectural Illustrations*, published in 1830, influenced hotel design for the next fifty years.

Six years later, Rogers designed New York's Astor

Above **A painting by J.A. Neubuys reflects the excitement caused by the arrival and**

departure of trains at the turn of the century. *Opposite* **The drawing room of the French**

Presidential train, photographed in 1946, with Lalique doors and splendid Art Deco

furniture by Franck. It was from such a car, in 1920, that France's President Deschanel

mysteriously disappeared to be found later walking round the French countryside in a

daze, attempting to convince disbelieving peasants of his rank.

Departure from Paddington Station by William Frith (1819–1909), 1861. Collection of Sir

Allen Lane, London. Paddington, in London, was the prototype for the great railroad stations of

Great Britain as well as the rest of the industrial world. It was the creation of the architect

Thomas Digby Wyatt and the engineer Isambard Kingdom Brunel, who was also the impresario

of the Great Western Railroad and the early mammoth transatlantic liners,

Great Western and ***Great Eastern.*** Paddington station was an outgrowth of the Universal

Exhibition of 1851, and still abuts the comfortable Great Western Hotel, one of the earliest of

the railroad station palaces, designed by Philip Charles Hardwick. Frith captures, in his famous

painting, the excitement of the railroad station as a social center, and conveys the lightness of

design of the magnificent iron and glass structure.

House, with twice as many rooms, improved lighting, heating, and hot-water plumbing. This was the first of many hotels built by the Astors; their later properties included two Waldorf-Astorias, the immense Hotel Astor on Broadway, with its large roof garden, and the St. Regis.

The denizens of American high society left their hot and dirty cities for the summer and set themselves up in such mountain resort areas as the Adirondacks, as well as Saratoga Springs, New York, and the New Jersey shore resorts of Cape May and Atlantic City. Saratoga Springs was the most fashionable place to be seen, and private railroad cars headed there filled with Vanderbilts, Goulds, Goelets, Diamond Jim Brady, and innumerable ladies of easy virtue. They stayed in vast new hotels such as the Grand Union and the United States, which had long, broad terraces from which a parade of elegant carriages bearing ladies in crinolines and gentlemen in spats and panama hats could be watched.

The four wings of the Gideon Putnam Hotel enclosed an opera house and a garden modeled on Paris's Tuileries. The gardens also contained a series of "cottages" with several bedrooms, a living room, and a dining room, where the super-rich could enjoy a degree of privacy not afforded by single rooms or

Color lithograph after a painting by Droz, showing the buffet of a railroad station in

1864. Before—and even after—the advent of the dining car, passengers took their

meals en route in quite elaborate dining rooms in Europe's railroad stations. Trains

stopped for as long as a few hours, and the quality of food and service in the first

class restaurants was extremely high. Here, a harassed waiter seems to be spilling a

bowl of soup to the amusement of the diners.

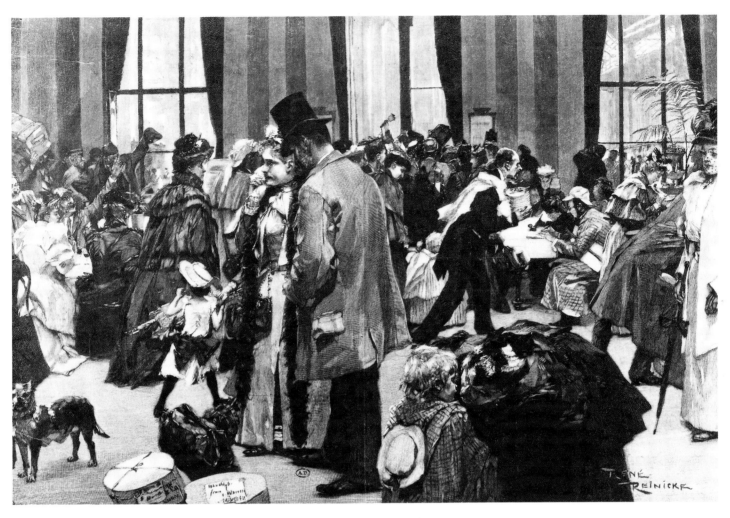

suites. Social climbers and businessmen on the make went to Saratoga Springs to meet the gilded few—who quickly left for Newport, where they built "cottages" as big and luxurious as Europe's castles.

Later in the century, there was a winter exodus to Florida, in particular to the Saint Augustine and Palm Beach resorts created by the enterprising railroad tycoon Henry Flagler, who had made his fortune in oil with John D. Rockefeller. Flagler's masterpiece was the Royal Poinciana in Palm Beach (1893), then the largest wooden structure in the world with room for 1,750 guests, who were transported the long distance from one end of the hotel to the other in "Afromobiles,"

Above A drawing by René Reinicke of the second class waiting room in Munich's Central Station. Each class was assigned separate rooms, which were generally quite comfortable, particularly as there were often long waits for—and between—trains. Munich's station was the heart of southern Germany's railroad hub, and an essential link to Austria and southern Europe, which explains the crowded conditions of its Biedermeier *Wartesaal.* Inaugurated in 1849, the station's architect, Friedrich Burklein, had been inspired by Paris's Gare de l'Est. *Below* This painting by Guillaume shows the rush for tickets in a railroad station.

A busy day at Paris's Gare St Lazare in 1910. This station was immortalized by Claude
Monet in his famous series of paintings of trains departing in clouds of steam. Located
equidistant from the Opera and the Parc Monceau, within walking distance of such
department stores as the Galeries Lafayette and the Printemps, the railroad's facilities
include a hotel with 350 beds, and a spectacular concourse. Its steel ribbing, designed
by Eugène Flachat, inspired the design of the Paris central market, Les Halles.

wicker chairs propelled by black cyclists, who sat behind so as not to spoil the view. It is no wonder that a British traveler, George Augustus Sala, wrote that "the American hotel is to an English hotel what an elephant is to a periwinkle ... as roomy as Buckingham Palace and not so much inferior in its fittings."

THE GRAND HOTEL IN EUROPE

After the middle of the nineteenth century, several factors spurred a colossal program of hotel building in Europe, a boom that has never been equaled and

which created most of the grand hotels that can still be enjoyed today. Railroads and transatlantic liners brought increasing quantities of tourists; the Industrial Revolution gave rise to a new bourgeoisie; and a wave of prosperity triggered the hotel boom. Finally, there were the universal exhibitions, which opened windows to technology, trade, and travel. P. C. Hardwick's Great Western Hotel (1852–54), at London's Paddington Station, might be considered the first attempt to create a luxury hotel in Europe. Built in the French Renaissance style, it has a royal waiting room where Queen Victoria rested before entraining for Windsor. Then came the Grosvenor (1860–61), next to Victoria Station, and the Charing Cross (1863–64).

The hordes of visitors to the 1862 International Exhibition encouraged the building of the Langham (1864), which was a true palace hotel up to American standards. It boasted rooms for four hundred guests, an Ambassadors' Audience Room, two libraries, and an elevator within its imposing, Italian Gothic–French Renaissance shell.

In Paris, Napoleon III encouraged financiers to put up large hotels for the many visitors to the French exhibitions. The first was the Grand Hôtel du Louvre on the Rue de Rivoli, built for the 1855 exhibition. This sober, classical structure was followed by the much larger and more extravagant Grand Hôtel (1862), opposite Garnier's opera house. It was a vast triangle

Above It is interesting to compare a photograph of Paddington Station in 1910 with William Frith's

painting of the station 50 years earlier. Nothing had changed architecturally but there was a great

difference in both the design and the quantity of trains in the station. The carriage had evolved, in

half a century, from an adaptation of the stage coach to the modern wagon we know today. *Below*

Despite advance in train design, passengers still arrived at the station in a horse and buggy,

although an early automobile already stands in line.

with seven hundred bedrooms ingeniously stacked on its three facades or inside the vast *cour*, and the large public rooms soared within the perimeter of the triangle itself. There were enormous ballrooms, a dining room embellished with sumptuous paintings and sculpture, and a domed *salon de thé*. The hotel displayed all the richness, vulgarity, and pomp of the *style Napoleon III*, as did the Continental (today the Intercontinental), whose grand salon was inspired by Garnier's foyer at the Opéra; it was built for the 1878 exhibition. Paris, like London, had a grand station hotel—the Hôtel du Palais d'Orsay, put up for the 1900 *Exposition*.

Great city hotels mushroomed in other cities; the Kaiserhof (1873–75) in Berlin, the Frankfurter Hof (1872–76), Munich's Vier Jahreszeiten (1856–57) and expanded Bayerischer Hof (1841), and Vienna's Britannia (1873) and Imperial (1865), the latter the former palace of the Duke of Württemberg. Resort hotels sprang up with equal speed, particularly in Switzerland. Resorts such as Lausanne-Ouchy and Lucerne later developed into cities, but their grand hotels were intended as summer residences for the idle rich. Lausanne's Beau Rivage (1861) remains one of the finest hotels in the world. The stock of hotels in Switzerland alone increased nearly threefold between 1894 and 1912.

Since the newly rich bourgeoisie wanted to live like princes, nineteenth-century hotels had to borrow the trappings of the royal palace of the previous century. With few exceptions, European grand hotels had long and noble facades, organized symmetrically and articulated with elements from the classic repertory. The balcony from which a royal family would have waved to its faithful subjects became the terrace of the hotel's grand suite. Other rooms had smaller terraces shaded

by striped awnings. The interior spaces had to be imposing, and palatial trappings included grand staircases, suites of corridors connecting public rooms, ballrooms derived from rooms of state, lavish dining rooms, and, occasionally, private theaters. Public rooms had to be of noble proportions, with large windows and an excess of stucco and statuary, frescoes and gilt: they were finished with crystal chandeliers, plush upholstery, and carpets copied by Aubusson on models made for royalty. A painted glass dome often crowned the main hall, which was filled with vast quantities of imitation-antique furniture and forests of potted palms. Liveried servants spoke in respectful and subservient terms to their temporary employers, the hotel's guests, as long as they paid their bills.

ocean frontage. There was an occasional attempt to accommodate local environmental features, but generally they were simply plunked down wherever their owners found a choice piece of real estate. The most obvious example of this indifference to the environment was the Maloja Palace Hotel (1882–84), a three-winged Italian neo-Renaissance pile set in a formal French garden in the middle of the rugged mountains of the Engadine and surrounded by Swiss peasant houses.

The high standard of comfort required in a palace

hotel meant incorporating the latest conveniences —from electric lights to telephones—and deluxe fittings. Sheets had to be linen, napkins had to be starched, tableware had to be the finest. But a hotel could never really be a palace without a few royals and aristocrats sprinkled around its public rooms.

NAMES AND LOCATIONS

Grand hotels were named to mark their aristocratic antecedents: Regina, Royal, Imperial, Majestic, Excelsior, Ermitage, and Splendide. Grand or Palace was really sufficient, but eager owners preferred the excessive redundancy of Majestic Palace, Royal Savoy, and even, in Nice, Grand Hôtel Excelsior Régina. There were many Victorias and Windsors, intimating that British royalty could be found in the corridors, and the many Hôtels d'Angleterre and de Londres insinuated cosmopolitan dignity, stability, and cleanliness. Parc, Bellevue, and Beau Rivage suggested a beautiful view, and there was a serious attempt to convey an international character; Deauville had the New Golf Hotel, Saint Petersburg the Hotel de l'Europe, Berlin the Boarding Palast, Joachimsthal in Czechoslovakia the Radium Palace, and Leysin, Switzerland, the Sanatorium Grand. A name like the Grande Albergo or Bolshoi Dvorets would have been considered déclassé.

The location of a grand hotel was terribly important. In town, the grand hotels eventually left the railroad stations for the new boulevards and lovely old squares. In resorts they were placed, if possible, in dominant positions—like the royal palace—or on lake and

CÉSAR RITZ

Coaxing these shy creatures into the open life of the hotel was the secret of the greatest hotelier of all time, César Ritz. He was born in 1850, to a poor family in a tiny Swiss mountain village. Throughout his astonishing career Ritz was haunted by his humble origins, but

The Hôtel Continental on the Rue Castiglione (now the Intercontinental),
like the Grand Hôtel or the Hôtel du Louvre, was put up by a syndicate to
accommodate visitors to Paris's *Expositions Universelles.* The elaborate and
theatrical decor used in these hotels is the perfect embodiment of the show and vulgarity that typified the prosperous
reign of Napoleon III and his Empress Eugénie. Fortunately, the decoration has mostly survived and is still the perfect
setting for grand parties as well as the fashion shows of Paris's leading couturiers.

not hampered by them. After a few menial jobs in small Swiss hotels he went to Paris for the 1876 exhibition and became a waiter at Voisin, where he learned his trade from the legendary maître d'hôtel Béllanger. There he came into contact with the grandees of the social, financial, and literary worlds, whom he served with distinction. A quick learner, Ritz graduated to maître d'hôtel at the Hôtel Splendide, where he served visiting millionaires such as Jay Gould, John Wanamaker, and Commodore Vanderbilt. The super-rich are often quite lonely, and Ritz knew how to listen, and to speak if spoken to. John Wanamaker counseled him to "Work hard and live an upright life," and Commodore Vanderbilt offered: "I kept my eyes open when I was a lad. You do the same and you'll get there too!" This high-sounding advice may have been helpful, but so was remembering which wines were preferred by J. P. Morgan, how Lady Furness liked her *entrecôte*, and what menu would please the Prince of Wales. As the young César worked his way through the luxurious restaurants and hotels of Europe, his face and manner soon became familiar to the nomads of golden travel, and his presence made them feel secure. It suddenly became chic to be able to say *"Bonjour, mon cher Ritz."*

The young César got a job as hotel manager of the Victoria in San Remo, where he increased the profits in one season from 17,000 to 70,000 francs. It was at this point that he was asked by Colonel Pfyffer von Altishofen to run the Grand Hôtel National in Lucerne, the most ornate and luxurious palace in Switzerland. The tale of the great success of their collaboration is told in detail in the next chapter.

After leaving the National, Ritz took over the Grand Hôtel de Monte Carlo in 1877 and applied the same magic to a far less splendid building. It was here that he first engaged Escoffier, the finest chef of his time. Together, Ritz and Escoffier created what may have been the best hotel restaurants ever and created dishes named after their illustrious clients as they moved from one grand hotel to the other. Some of these were Salade Réjane, Poires Mary Garden, Poularde Adelina Patti, Fraises Sarah Bernhardt, Poulet Tetrazzini, and both Pêche Melba and Melba Toast. When Ritz took over the London Savoy with Escoffier in the kitchen,

his friend the Prince of Wales came to the opening. This was a revolutionary occurrence in hidebound Victorian England, where the royal family was treated with the same reverence as the pope in Rome. The prince was free to do as he liked abroad, but dining in public within the shadow of Buckingham Palace was quite another matter. There were astonished gasps, but from then on there was no duke or duchess who worried about the indignity of dining in a public place.

THE LONDON RITZ
Ritz founded his first British hotel—the new Carlton—at the bottom of London's Haymarket in 1899, having established a fabulous reputation for himself in London when managing the Savoy Room from 1889 to 1896 for D'Oyly Carte. During his time there he had done much to change the way in which London hotels were perceived, transforming those under his control from simple sleeping bases into recognizable social, entertainment, and culinary centers. Most other British hotels founded in the period were based on his model, and his influence certainly extended to the newly opened Claridge's in 1894, for which, as part of the Savoy group, he helped to set the tone.

Hotels such as the Excelsior Regina in Nice, the Majestic and the Meurice (*opposite*) in Paris, epitomized the palace hotel which was an invention of the Belle Epoque. The Meurice's dining room, beautifully lit and overlooking the Rue de Rivoli and the Tuileries, demonstrates the borrowing of the trappings of the Royal Palace, including frescoed ceilings, heavy chandeliers, and marble pilasters with gilded Corinthian capitals. In the grand hotel, everybody could be king for a price.

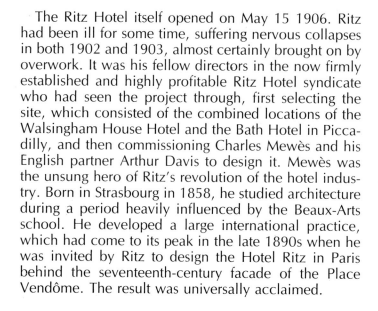

The Ritz Hotel itself opened on May 15 1906. Ritz had been ill for some time, suffering nervous collapses in both 1902 and 1903, almost certainly brought on by overwork. It was his fellow directors in the now firmly established and highly profitable Ritz Hotel syndicate who had seen the project through, first selecting the site, which consisted of the combined locations of the Walsingham House Hotel and the Bath Hotel in Piccadilly, and then commissioning Charles Mewès and his English partner Arthur Davis to design it. Mewès was the unsung hero of Ritz's revolution of the hotel industry. Born in Strasbourg in 1858, he studied architecture during a period heavily influenced by the Beaux-Arts school. He developed a large international practice, which had come to its peak in the late 1890s when he was invited by Ritz to design the Hotel Ritz in Paris behind the seventeenth-century facade of the Place Vendôme. The result was universally acclaimed.

For the London site, Mewès and Davis presented plans not only for the structure and exterior, but also for a thematic decorative style throughout the hotel's interior in the Louis XVI mode. By this time Ritz, who would normally have controlled every detail himself, had suffered such a recession in his health that the architects were left with almost unhampered responsibility: it was fortunate for the syndicate that they appointed, in Mewès, someone who, after years of working with him, knew Ritz's mind (probably, during this period, better than Ritz knew it himself).

M. Malley was the first chef to make an impact at the London Ritz, with Escoffier directing operations

Above right The terrace restaurant of the Paris Ritz, used mostly for afternoon tea, was an oasis of calm in the middle of the city.

Below right The Grand Dining Room, photographed in the days of Marcel

Proust who was faithfully served by Olivier. Note the Louis XV style that was so favored by Ritz and Mewès.

Above left Ritz's great supporter Bertie.

institution. A stickler for cleanliness, he did away with heavy damasks and brocade in bedrooms, as he felt they harbored germs, and replaced them with muslin and paint. He installed marble bathrooms in every room at the Paris Ritz (its competition, the Bristol, had one per floor). He invented indirect lighting, using

from Paris, and acting as a consultant, advisor, and setter of standards. The first Manager was Henry Elles, an old colleague of Ritz's from his Savoy days, who, in Ritz's decline, managed both the London hotel and the Vendôme. After initial problems—mainly concerning the plumbing and the innovatory air-conditioning system—the hotel took off to a great success, sealed, as ever in Ritz's career, by the patronage of His Highness the Prince of Wales: where he went, others were sure to follow soon, and thus the rich and powerful in the land, together with vast numbers of foreign statesmen, dignitaries, ambassadors, and wealthy travelers, quickly adopted it as their favored London center.

RITZ'S LEGACY
Ritz's innovations were crucial to the grand hotel as an

alabaster, wall moldings, and glass, and made pink-shaded light the dominant color for intimate settings. He became the first superstar hotelier by fulfilling the hotel's potential as a social center and bringing the great restaurant into the orbit of hostelry. With Charles Mewès he created a specific decorative style that could immediately be identified with a Ritz hotel, an idea that is immensely important today as old hotels become inexorably integrated into chains and new hotels are created in a preconceived style. Most important of all, his Ritz Hotel Development Company created the first international licensing arrangements in the business. That is why many great hotels around the world still bear the Ritz name, although some would no longer meet with the founder's high standards.

The grand hotel existed before Ritz carved his first roast and continues its proud tradition even to this day, but under César Ritz this wonderful institution reached its apogee.

Above left **The London Ritz.** *Above right* **The Royal Suite of the Paris Ritz decorated in the Empire style, on the *étage noble*, with French windows looking over the Place Vendôme.**

THE GRAND TOUR

Louis Vuitton bags ready for a voyage. The cap, gloves and goggles indicate

that a racy couple is about to step into a newfangled automobile. Isadora

Duncan's scarf, much like the one wrapped around the woman's hat, caught

in the spokes of a car driven along the coast road in the south of France by

her poet husband Sergei Ysenine, and strangled her to death. We trust the

owners of this luggage had better luck.

A man who has not been in Italy is always conscious of an inferiority from his not having seen what it is expected a man should see. The grand object of travelling is to see the shores of the Mediterranean.

Dr. Johnson

Before rushing off to such exotic places as Istanbul, Cairo, Bombay or Port Arthur, the average rich American or Englishman, as well as the newly rich of the Continent, could now explore closer to home with far greater ease than their grandfathers had. In the eighteenth century, the grand tourists went from London to Naples via France and Switzerland and returned through south Germany, Austria and the Low Countries. In the golden age of travel, time was telescoped by the railway, comfort provided by the grand hotel, and disease reduced by Dr. Lister. But for the grand tourist, neither the itinerary nor the purpose—education and enlightenment—of the tour were very different in the nineteenth century to what they had been a hundred years earlier.

The adventurous English, as always, set the pace, and their goal was Italy. Every upper-class British schoolboy had learned Latin and Greek at his public (i.e., private) school and was eager to see the Rome of the Caesars and the Florence of the Renaissance. Italy's Renaissance and baroque palaces and churches were among the greatest monuments of Western civilization, and the treasures of her museums were endless.

English and Americans also had great interest in bringing back such works of art as could be pried off the palace walls of the spendthrift Italian nobility. In the eighteenth century Consul Smith in Venice sent England countless Guardis, Titians, and Tintorettos, and at the end of the nineteenth century Lord Duveen, aided by Bernard Berenson, hunted down every available Italian masterpiece for his rich American clients. The English and Americans could afford the best and were willing to pay; it is to these grand tourists and dealers that we owe the incredible collections of such dukes as Devonshire and Bedford, most of the masterpieces in the national galleries of London and Washington, and the delights of smaller museums instituted by the likes of Henry Clay Frick in New York and Isabella Stewart Gardner in Boston. To track down and capture a great painting (or in the case of William Randolph Hearst, an entire castle) was the ultimate shopping experience.

Above A poster advertising PLM's service from France to Belgium through Switzerland and Italy, basically the nineteenth-century version on rails of the eighteenth-century grand tour on Europe's rugged roads. Clockwise from the top are the harbor at Genoa, the National Temple in Turin, the Isola Bella at Stresa and a view of the Alps, which were now cut through by train tunnels. In the center is Milan's Piazza del Duomo with its Gothic Cathedral. *Opposite* The English were the grandest of tourists and Claridge's on Upper Brook Street received the grandest of foreign visitors. A panel of the Isola Bella, set off by palm trees, was inset above one of the hotel's radiators to add warmth to Britain's foggy winter.

TRAVEL BEFORE THE GOLDEN AGE

The young eighteenth-century aristocrat's grand tour was a three- or four-year opportunity to learn other languages, become less provincial, and return home with the broadened horizon needed for his preordained role as leader of a fixed and stratified society. He traveled with a personal servant and a tutor (called a "bear") whose job was to guide, protect, and instruct. Europe was full of thieves and highwaymen; one never traveled alone or at night, and was well advised not to take off one's spurs aboard ship to avoid their being stolen during seasickness. Travelers carried food to assuage their hunger (and keep off starving dogs), checked for secret doors concealing thieves, kept their money in their socks, strapped down their baggage, and watched out for crooked customs of-

ficials. And staying healthy was a serious problem. Paris and Venice were filled with ladies of easy virtue; smallpox and venereal diseases were easily caught and nearly always fatal.

A grand tour always started at one of the Channel ports, usually Dover. In the eighteenth century the trip there from London took a whole day and five changes of horses, and an overnight stay in one of the filthy Channel ports could make one eager to depart. Early the next morning, a rowboat negotiated the rough seas to the packet boat, which would reach Calais in three to six hours, depending on the winds. At Calais, after an unpleasant customs inspection, the grandest tourists would get into their own carriages for the week-long trip to Paris. Others would have a choice between a *carrosse* or a *coche*, known in English as a diligence.

The Coast by Pierre Outin, exhibited in the Salon of 1893. The diligence was the most popular carriage for traveling around Europe in the pre-train era and was portrayed in many nineteenth- century European paintings. The passengers here are taking a rest on a long trip, and seem to be confronted by beggars and local mutts. There was always the risk of robbers and highwaymen, particularly on the coastal roads between France and Italy.

The *carrosse* carried six passengers; the larger and heavier *coche* accommodated sixteen and had two large wicker baskets for trunks, other baggage, and even excess passengers (period drawings also show travelers on the roof).

To facilitate communication, people traveled with books containing useful phrases in several languages, much as they do today. *The Gentleman's Pocket Companion for Travelling into Foreign Ports* contained the following dialogue in French, German and Italian between the tourist and a chambermaid at an Inn:

"Shall we be well lodged with you for this night?"

"Yes, very well, Sir."

"Have you good stable, good hay, good oats, good litter, good wine?"

"The best."

"Sweetheart, is my bed made? Is it good, clean, warm?"

"Yes, sir, it is a good featherbed. The sheets are very clean."

"Where is the chamber pot? Where is the privy?"

"Follow me and I will show you the way. Go straight up and you will find it on your right hand: if you see it not you will soon smell it. Sir, do you want anything else?"

"Yes, my dear, put out the candle and come closer to me." Little else needs to be said about contemporary conditions.

The agreeable part of the trip was a slow progression through the lush countryside of northern France, with time to explore the abbeys of Normandy and Brittany and the Gothic cathedrals of Caen and Bayeux, to study medieval towns and visit Rouen, Amiens, and Reims, where Dom Pérignon had discovered the secret of making champagne. The direct post-route to Paris went through Chantilly where the tourist could visit the castle and gardens of the Prince de Condé and—with luck—see "Les très riches heures du Duc de Berry," the finest medieval breviary ever created. France and England shared so much history that a young gentleman's tutor worked overtime discoursing on William the Conqueror and Joan of Arc.

TO PARIS IN LUXURY CLASS

The travelers of Messrs. Pullman and Nagelmackers went about things quite differently, whizzing in the morning through the English or French countryside sipping drinks in their comfortable plush compartments, reposing their heads on an antimacassar. They could also be found in the dining car, being waited upon by footmen in pumps, knee breeches and livery, as a chef produced one course after the other from his tiny kitchen. The clickety-clack of wheels and the train's hypnotic sway relieved all anxiety; passengers quickly made friends with newfound table companions. The only compromise with movement was an engraved crystal wine tumbler—a stemmed glass might be knocked over in a sudden stop. The passenger boarded a comfortable ferry from a commodious dock very close to the railroad; the conductor would go along to make sure that everything went smoothly. On the other side of the Channel another luxury train would speed to Paris in a few hours.

The king of the London–Paris run, however, was Lord Dalziel, who in 1908 had bought the assets of the British Pullman Car Co., which he was to operate with great flair as his own company. Dalziel made the trip a sheer delight unless it was spoiled by a rough crossing. Unlike the blue CIWL cars, Pullman's were painted in the most luscious brown and cream, like a splendid chocolate sundae. By the 1920s, Dalziel had done away with the traditional dining car, and meals were served to passengers as they sat on large, blue-patterned armchairs —*face à face*—with a mahogany table between them. The baggage racks were polished brass, the carpets deep and purple, the walls were embellished with Art-Deco marquetry. Identical trains were used on each side of the Channel so that the passenger felt a continuity in his voyage. Most thought that the train had been shipped on a separate steamer! In fact, passengers stepped off the "Golden Arrow" in Dover to step on to the "Flèche d'Or" in Calais. The next step was obvious. The trip started in London or Paris after dinner instead of in the early morning, and one went to bed in a comfortable sleeping compartment which was put onto a channel ferry, waking up just before pulling into Victoria Station in London or the Gare du Nord in Paris. This service was started in 1936 and still continues today.

PARIS

A visit to Paris was very different for the eighteenth-century grand tourist than it was for the grandees of the Belle Epoque. The best hotels used to be in the Faubourg St. Germain outside the city walls, but most tourists stayed long enough to take furnished rooms or board with a private family. The first order of business for an eighteenth-century gentleman was to get rid of his plain English clothes and buy a splendid French wardrobe—powdered wigs, ruffles, suits of brilliantly colored cut velvet, pumps, jeweled buckles for his shoes, or gold handled sword and endless other finery. (In the Belle Epoque, the reverse was true as elegant Frenchmen crossed the channel to be dressed by the tailors of Savile Row.) The splendidly equipped English gentleman now set out to explore the city. The Belle Epoque tourist would have been dazzled by the great new boulevards of Baron Haussman. His ancestor was somewhat horrified by the runaway carriages splashing mud from the gutters that ran right down the middle of the narrow streets. Paris then had a greater population than Istanbul or London and was incredibly noisy. But all generations enjoyed the beautiful bridges over the Seine, the tree-lined Champs Elysées, the formal gardens of the Tuileries, the Luxembourg and the Palais Royal, the imposing classical facade of the Louvre, as well as Notre Dame and Versailles. The early tourist would have seen the king and queen, who were very accessible, and could have admired their splendid royal furnishings. His great-grandson would have found Versailles emptied by his father's friends who had bought the masterpieces of Oeben, Riesner and Carlin for a pittance after the French Revolution.

Curiously, the eighteenth-century traveler complained endlessly about French food, which was then very inferior. It was overseasoned, and the meat was tough and badly carved. Water from the Seine gave the English what is now referred to as Delhi belly or Montezuma's revenge. Clearly, Carême was not only a great chef but a revolutionary, as gastronomy became a highlight of later visits to Paris.

The English of all generations also complained that the French were rude, arrogant and xenophobic to the extreme, but intellectuals from Walpole to Oscar Wilde were dazzled by the brilliance of conversation in the salons of the city. The educated and curious, such as Dr. Johnson or James Boswell, visited the picture galleries in the Palais Royal, churches, courts of justice, the king's natural history museum and the great libraries of the capital. Sybaritic young gentlemen rose late, had their wigs powdered, and went about the city by coach and to the English coffee house where they made plans for the evening. These generally included dinner in a tavern, then seeing a play in one of the famous theaters of the capital followed perhaps by a visit to one of the finer brothels of the city, the two best being run by Mme. Charlotte Genevieve Heugeut.

After the French Revolution, the educated met in the new Great Gallery of the Louvre, which had already established itself as the world's most encyclopedic museum. Napoleon's conquests had added immeasurably to the riches amassed by France's kings, and Champollion's excavations in Egypt brought the treasures of the pharaohs to the museum.

The Belle Epoque provided other reasons to visit Paris: the *Expositions Universelles* and the new *grands magasins*, or department stores, which were offshoots of these world's fairs. The great Paris exhibitions took place in 1855, 1867, 1878, 1889, and 1900. The year 1925 saw the famous exhibition of modern, industrial, and decorative arts, which featured what is now known as the Art Deco style. These important events inspired many landmarks. The Grand Hôtel du Louvre

Above The dining car of the Sud-Express, which ran between Paris and Madrid via Irún, in 1907, and was built by Ringhoffer in Prague. In luxury expresses before World War I, a servant's livery often included knee breeches and buckled shoes. When the service started, the waiters even wore wigs, but the clients complained that the powder was dusting their food. *Opposite* A painting by Louis Beraud (1852–1930) of the central dome of the *Exposition Universelle* of 1889. The exhibition hall was known as the "Pavillon des Beaux Arts," and was designed by Jean-Camille Formige (1845–1926). The extensive use of large areas of glass was inspired by Paxton's Crystal Palace, and the Arabs in costume convey the new interest in travel and the exotic.

was built for the 1855 exposition; the Hôtel Continental (now Intercontinental) for the one in 1878; the Eiffel Tower for the centennial in 1889; and the Hôtel du Quai d'Orsay, the Grand and Petit Palais, as well as the Pont Alexandre III, for the one in 1900.

Expositions celebrated international progress in art and industry and also frankly advertised products, including the latest Baccarat and St-Louis crystal, Christofle silver, Haviland and Sèvres porcelain, and many other expensive and fashionable commodities.

SHOPPING

By the mid-nineteenth century France was the leader in fashion and luxury products. Parisian designers and craftsmen set the style for the whole world. For the rich of all nations, Paris became a shopper's paradise. In her magnificent department stores one could buy—not just admire—the wonders featured at the expositions. The Bon Marché came in 1862–72, La Samaritaine in 1870, Les Grands Magasins du Louvre in 1877, Au Printemps in 1881. These temples of consumerism set the tone for retailing from New York to Saint Petersburg. Inspired by the lacy steel-and-glass webbing of Britain's Crystal Palace, Paris's department stores were vast, luminous cathedrals displaying mountains of wonderful wares. Shopping kept the ladies there all day; to divert their husbands or lovers, Bon Marché had a billiard room, a reading room, and a buffet, and also offered music, foreign language courses, and fencing instruction. Amenities were to be found in other stores as well. The reading room of the Grands Magasins du Louvre was as luxurious as Empress Eugénie's salons. Its walls and ceilings dripped with carved putti and caryatids; its carpeted floors were packed with potted palms.

While their husbands were otherwise occupied, the *very* rich women went to the exclusive salons of Poiret and Worth—who dressed all the queens of the Second Empire. These were the first dressmakers to elevate themselves to the rank of couturier.

Dressed by the couturiers, the most elegant foreigners entered the whirl of the season. Society in Paris blossomed for a short period in mid-June, like an exotic plant that then suddenly disappeared into a long hibernation. There were lunch parties, teas, dinners and balls given by the Duke and Duchess of Vendôme, the Prince and Princess Murat, the Marquise de Talleyrand and the Rothschilds, who were the only Jews to make the scene in a major way. They entertained in their palaces on the Rue de Courcelles and the Rue Lafitte, and received guests outside Paris at Ferrières, a staggeringly luxurious pile of a château built by Paxton and filled with great treasures of art. Even visiting monarchs felt poor when visting the ugly Baron James.

Between receptions, the rich English and Americans went with their horse and carriage to the Bois de

---

Above **The Dome of Les Galeries Lafayette in Paris, founded in 1895.** *Opposite* **A fabric shop in Paris about 1860. The City of Lights reigned supreme as the shopping capital of the world, and its new department stores were cathedrals of commerce. The stores were a way of life that enticed the rising middle classes who read, rested, ate, listened to music, and took courses in foreign languages and fencing in between shopping for the latest fashions and furniture featured at the** *Expositions Universelles.*

Boulogne where they met Russian princes, maharajas, kings and cocottes taking a breath of fresh air, then went skating at the Palais des Glâce. The beau monde stayed at the Ritz on Place Vendome, which had been transformed by Ritz and Mewès in 1898 from a great *hotel particulier* designed by Mansart—then occupied by the Credit Mobilier—into the most exquisite of small hotels. Those less fortunate stayed at the Hotel Bristol on the Faubourg St. Honoré or in the new hotels on the Grands Boulevards. When there was no great ball to attend, everybody went to the theater to see the reigning star, Sarah Bernhardt, and then repaired to Maxim's for a late champagne supper in the most beautiful Art Nouveau decor ever created. And to recover, they left with a steamer trunk to spend the weekend in Dieppe, Le Touquet or Deauville.

THE CÔTE D'AZUR

In the eighteenth century, the route south ran toward Lyons and the Mediterranean coast. From Lyons some grand tourists hurried on to Switzerland and then crossed the Alps into Italy. Others avoided the terrors of Alpine passes by going to Marseilles, where ferries connected to Genoa and Leghorn, or to Nice, from which they took the rough coast road winding through the Ligurian Alps. It was not much of a choice. The Mediterranean was swarming with Barbary pirates, the coast road was filled with bandits, and there was little pleasure in Nice, Cannes, or Monte Carlo, which had, according to a traveler in 1785, "two or three streets upon precipitous rocks; eight hundred witches dying of hunger; a tumble-down castle; and a battalion of French troops."

Life in Paris at the turn of the century set the tone for all the civilized world. *Above* Diners on the Hotel Meurice's roof garden. This contemporary advertisement boasts of "the freshness of beautiful summer nights, the sky twinkling with shining stars . . . electricity glistening from small lampshades and sweet smelling flowers on the tables. We are two steps from the Place de la Concorde and yet one feels so far away." *Opposite* The beau monde takes the air in 1900 on the Avenue du Bois. Displaying one's finery in splendid carriages was a favorite occupation of the rich from Saratoga to Cairo.

Less than a century later, in 1883, Georges Nagelmackers banished such gloom with his Calais–Nice–Rome luxury service. It was not altruism but business that motivated him: by then, royal patronage had made the Côte d'Azur a winter playground. The season lasted from December to March, and Monte Carlo became the most fashionable winter resort of the Belle Epoque, thanks to François Blanc.

MONACO

By 1840, François and his twin brother, Louis, had made a fortune with their casino in Bad Homburg. In 1856, Monaco opened its first casino—two rooms at the Villa Bellevue—and François, who bought the concession in 1863, founded the Société des Bains de Mer, the SBM, which quickly became the power in Monaco. A match to François' vision was the extraordinary determination of his German wife, Marie Hansel, who had a flair for the arts and society—she married off one daughter to Prince Radziwill and the

other to Prince Roland Bonaparte. Together François and Marie quickly turned Monte Carlo from an abandoned rockpile into the greatest gambler's paradise of its time. The first true casino was built by Godineau de la Bretonnerie between 1856 and 1862. In 1872 Dutrou added a Moorish room and the terraces from which ruined gamblers would leap to the railroad tracks below, and in 1878 the entire casino was overhauled by Charles Garnier, the genial architect of the Paris Opéra. Its interiors are a coffee-colored confection highlighted in gold. It has been preserved as one of the finest Belle Epoque buildings.

César Ritz started running the Grand Hôtel de Monte Carlo in 1881, but it was the Hôtel de Paris, built in 1862, that dominated the magnificent new Place du Casino. Its hall, whose domed ceiling was covered with stucco tortoises, was the meeting place of generations of gamblers who fortified themselves in the superb restaurant, a gilded hive of Napoleonic bees. A contemporary traveler reminisced about these days in her memoirs:

> Monte Carlo was a glamorous place where money lost its normal value; the tables were piled with gold and silver pieces which came and went at the caprice of a whirling ball or the colour of a card. The days were made lovely by the sun, the sea, the great baskets full of carnations, stocks and roses offered for sale by sunburnt, smiling women, and the perpetual smell of freshly-ground coffee which came from the service door of the Hôtel de Paris, where a man in a blue blouse sat roasting it and singing a gay song, added to the fascination.

There was a whiff of scandal about Monte Carlo. Distraught gamblers swallowed poison or shot themselves in the suites of the Hôtel de Paris (presumably the terraces were crowded); even Sarah Bernhardt attempted to do away with herself with barbiturates. Every courtesan took rooms in the grand hotels, and scandal-sensitive Queen Victoria lowered the shades of her train compartment as she went through "Monte" en route to Cimiez.

In 1907, the French Parliament—sensing a good thing—agreed to the opening on the Riviera of other

Monte Carlo was *the* place in Europe to have fun in at the turn of the century. *Above* The terrace of the Hotel Ermitage. *Left* A poster by Hugo d'Ales enticing tourists to visit the more staid Menton. *Opposite* The terrace of the Café de la Paix on the Place du Casino in Monte Carlo. The overcoats and parasols indicate that this is a bright day at the height of the mid-winter season. Ladies of the time protected their fair skin from even the weak rays of the winter sun. Sun worship started only after World War I (*overleaf*).

carried back mimosa and carnations to decorate the ballrooms of Imperial Russia's aristocratic palaces when the winter season was in full swing. Evening dress was *de rigeur* and there was dancing on the train as it made its way through the wintry night, as there was on the Cote d'Azur Pullman which devoted an entire car to the turkey trot and Charleston as of 1929. The cars of this Paris–Nice Express were truly splendid, its glass panels made by Lalique, its cut velvet upholstery and marquetry panelling of unusual beauty. A ballet, commissioned by Serge Diaghilev, as well as Agatha Christie's *The Mystery of the Blue Train*, published in 1928, immortalized this legendary train made up exclusively of Wagon Lits cars. The ballet produced by Diaghilev in 1924 was a spoof on the new interest in golf, tennis and racing: it was titled "Train Bleu" after the train itself.

casinos, ending Monte Carlo's virtual monopoly. Soon, gambling was all over the coast and there were magnificent casinos in Nice, Cannes, Beaulieu and Menton. The shore-line of the lovely Mediterranean became the contemporary equivalent of the Las Vegas "Strip".

Gamblers and pleasure seekers came from all over Europe, and from far away Russia they travelled south aboard the Saint Petersburg—Vienna—Nice—Cannes Express complete with card-tables and a reading room, which brought Grand Dukes to the gaming tables and

SWITZERLAND

This temporary excursion to the decadence of the Côte d'Azur, however, has temporarily distracted us from our destination—Naples via the Alps. In the eighteenth century, most travelers would continue in their coach from Lyons to the Swiss border at Vallorde. They would seek out Voltaire in Calvinist Geneva where he had settled on an estate in nearby Ferney (now called

Above A reception and ball in the restaurant of the Hotel de Paris, Monte Carlo, in 1930. This magnificent palace hotel, right

next to the casino, vied with Ritz's Grand Hotel for elegant and fashionable guests. The Great Depression appears not to

have affected the life style of Europe's rich who continued in grand style while their American counterparts jumped out of

windows or suffered the privations of prohibition. *Above center* A brochure, printed for the 1922–23 winter season,

advertising the Calais-Méditerranée Express, one of many trains that brought tourists to the Côte d'Azur. It shows the

interior arrangements of the sleeping cars which became salons by day and bedrooms at night.

Ferney Voltaire) just outside the city limits, or they would visit Mme de Stael at her chateau in Coppet. Lausanne and the nearby Château de Chillon on the beautiful Lac Léman later attracted the likes of Lord Byron who swam long distances in its cold waters before settling down for the evening at the Hôtel d'Angleterre in Ouchy to write his ode to freedom, "The Prisoner of Chillon". From Lausanne, the eighteenth-century grand tourist would go to Basel via

Neuchâtel, where, if extremely well connected or persistent, he could meet Jean-Jacques-Rousseau in the 1760s. Basel was then the largest city in Switzerland but only had two fine buildings, both belonging to a local banker. The smaller Zurich was a deadly bore where social life started at tea-time and ended before dinner; the city's gates were closed often before sunset, sumptuary laws were still operating in the 1780s, and there was little to keep the tourist, particularly as life in towns was quite expensive. In contrast, the sparklingly fresh countryside offered a paradise for wanderers in search of the simple, natural life. But the admiration of nature was an invention of the Age of Romanticism, so no eighteenth-century gentleman was interested in reveling in the rugged beauty of Switzerland's ever-present mountains, its rushing streams and rivers or its many deep lakes.

MOUNTAINS AND VALETS

It was precisely these natural resources that made Switzerland a summer mecca for grandees of the Belle Epoque. In the second half of the nineteenth century, there was no sun worship, a tanned skin being the attribute of a toiling peasant not of the elegant lady or gentleman. Ladies shaded themselves from the summer sun with silk parasols whose handles were often of gold, enameled by Fabergé or Cartier. Gentlemen protected their faces with straw boaters, Panama hats or even toppers. The hotels of the Côte d'Azur were boarded up in May, and César Ritz's staff at the Grand Hôtel de Monte Carlo took the third class train up to the Grand Hôtel National in Lucerne, which he had made into one of the most magnificent palaces in Europe.

The National, designed in 1870, was Ritz's first great success. It was built and belonged to the distinguished Swiss Colonel Pfyffer d'Altishofer who had been Grand Chamberlain at the Court of the King of Naples. The hotel's gigantic rooms and frescoed ceilings reflected the Colonel's life at court, but the service was not up to the architecture and the establishment quickly ran into trouble. As previously mentioned, Pfyffer hired Ritz who brought his magic touch and his chic followers. The food improved, the service was impeccable and during July and August the National was the place to be, packed with the usual crowned heads, opera singers, American tycoons and Italian countesses. Ritz organized balls, boating parties, hunts, concerts and a weekly cotillion which was straight out of Proust (one of Ritz's most devoted clients, always served dinner late at night on the Place Vendôme by the famous Olivier, who lit a fire for him and carefully closed the padded doors to keep out drafts.) In her memoirs, Marie Louise Ritz evokes a party organized by Ritz at the National to celebrate the betrothal in 1885 of Count Trapani's daughter, Princess Caroline de Bourbon, to the Polish Count André Zamoyski. There was a delicious dinner followed by dancing and at midnight a signal was given and everybody moved to the terrace.

'But it is Naples!' 'But it is Versailles!' were some of the delighted and conflicting cries of pleasure that

The season in Switzerland was in full swing during the summer months. The mountain and lake resorts were linked by such luxurious trains as the Golden Mountain Pullman Express, seen above c.1925. The narrow-gauge railway ran between Montreaux and Zweisemmen. The platforms were lined with liveried porters from the great hotels, who met guests, helped them with their bags and transported them to grand hotels. On the right is the head porter from the Schweizenhof in Zurich.

These monuments to luxurious living are still with us, although as Swiss resorts developed into towns they have become in many cases city hotels. Among the most magnificent are the Beau Rivage in Lausanne-Ouchy, with its sublime oak-filled park and dog cemetery, or the Montreux-Palace, whose public rooms, with their traditional white and gold carved plaster crowd of naked buxom ladies, angels and mythological gods and goddesses, were the equal of those in the great hotels of Paris and London. Both hotels were used for a series of international conferences when great statesmen carved up both Europe and Asia as waiters in white tie and tails cut up the game they had ordered. To this period we owe the Beau Rivage in Geneva, the Baur au Lac and Dolder in Zurich and the gigantic palace hotels of such glorious mountain resorts as Grindelwald and Kandersteg.

were heard. . . . Around the lake shores illuminated fountains played. And upon the surface of the lake moved fifty sailboats, like miniature coloured fires, duplicated in the dark waters. For, as the guests were seen to descend the flight of stairs on to the green terrace, a sailor in each boat set off Bengal lights and Roman candles. Among the smaller boats a larger boat sailed proudly, carrying at its prow an enormous lantern—there were 1,000 candles in it!—upon the luminous parchment shade of which was painted the linked arms of the Bourbon and Zamoyski families. As the last Roman candle exploded, the last Bengal light faded out into nothing, a Neapolitan quartet in one of the boats struck up 'O sole mio.'

Wagner, in his nearby villa at Treibischen would have preferred the "Liebestod."

The next morning, as the embers cooled on the mountain-top fires that had been lit to enhance the moonlight serenade, many of the Italian grandees stepped into their waiting private railroad cars that were attached to the direct Paris–Rome express through the new Simplon Tunnel. We must presume that the regular travelers waited patiently while the plush cars were attached. Rank, in the Belle Epoque, had its privileges. The National was the prototype of the large and luxurious lake-side Swiss hotel whose comfort and very presence was a "raison de voyage."

THE ALPS AND ITALY

Eighteenth-century grand tourists of every rank had a rough time crossing the Alps. By 1817, there was a route *over* the Simplon; it required a three A.M. start and eight hours of trekking, and included the risk of avalanches and flash floods during thaws. Travelers descended by wheelbarrow or sled, depending on the season. Earlier travelers had it worse, generally going over the terrifying Mount Cenis wrapped in furs, carried in a straw sedan chair by four porters who leaped over crevasses and rocks. When conditions deteriorated, everybody got down and crawled.

In March, travelers descending from the passes —then as now—come upon the first blossoming fruit trees embellishing the shores of Lake Maggiore on the Lombard plain. This is the land where Goethe's *Orangen* bloomed, a place of endless delights. The rigidity of Switzerland is suddenly replaced with humanism, the provincialism of the canton with the grandeur of the principality as one turns a corner and comes upon the first man-made wonder: docked in the blue waters of the lake, opposite Stresa, is a great stone galleon whose stern is the baroque palace of Prince Borromeo

The hotel car of the Hotel Riche-Mont, now Richmond, near the shores of the Lac Léman in Geneva. The Armleders, who founded this luxury hotel, are one of Switzerland's dynastic hotellerie families—like the Badrutts of the Palace Hotel in Saint Moritz. They created a standard of lodging that was the basis for luxury hotels throughout the world.

Winter Sports

Season 1923-4

THOS. COOK & SON.

WINTER SPORT

THOS. COOK & SON

and whose prow is a multilayered garden of exotic plants and trees connected by marble staircases decked with statues. Built in the seventeenth century, this fantasy proclaims the genius of Italy to all who travel the beautiful lakeside road. In 1913, the Grand Hôtel des Iles Borromés was built right opposite the Isola Borromeo. For many years it was the only hotel on this part of the road, and its golden book has been signed by its many grand guests, from Queen Victoria on down. Thanks to this hotel, Stresa quickly became a popular summer resort and not just a stopping-off place on the way to Milan.

Winter sports started to come into vogue only between the two world wars and were largely a scheme to fill Switzerland's luxury palaces in the winter. A few hardy souls did attempt to ski down the mountains after climbing up with seal-skins attached to their narrow planks. Skating, sledding and tobogganing were more popular activities, with the British—as usual—leading the pack. They created the Cresta run in Saint Moritz, the Mecca of bob-sledders and tobogganers, an activity whose danger is surpassed only by Grand Prix racing. *Above* A group in the 1930s tobogganing in Chamonix.

TROIS COURONNES
VEVEY

MILAN

Milan was enjoyed by early tourists for the many masterpieces in the famous cabinet of Signor Manfredo Settalo, which was the backbone of the Brera; for Leonardo da Vinci's *Last Supper* in the church of Santa Maria della Grazie (seventeenth-century visitors were already remarking on its poor condition); and for its splendid Duomo, begun in 1386, and not finished for about five hundred years. At that point it was announced that the cathedral urgently needed major repairs; ''building the Duomo'' became local vernacular for any hopeless, Sisyphean task. The glory of Milan as of 1778 was the Teatro alla Scala, the high altar of Italian opera. This splendid neoclassical structure, whose white and gold auditorium has perfect acoustics, was a mecca for music lovers, particularly in the late nineteenth and early twentieth centuries, when Arturo Toscanini ruled it with an iron hand. Many of the operas of Puccini, Mascagni, and even Verdi had their premieres here. Ricordi published the scores from his office downtown; Caruso, Melba, Patti, and the de Reszke brothers stayed at the Hotel Marino alla Scala across the street; Maestro Toscanini held court at his mansion a block away on Via Durini; and everybody met at Bice to argue interpretation, sets, and casting over plates of *risotto alla Milanese*. After the opera, the devotees—in white tie and top hats, their ladies covered in splendid jewelry—wandered over to the restaurants in the Galleria, another Belle Epoque iron-and-glass wonder. Impresarios arrived by express from Paris, Berlin, and Vienna, always on the lookout for fresh talent and new operas. Gatti-Casazza and Otto Kahn of New York's Metropolitan Opera came aboard transatlantic liners, as did the impresarios of the Teatro Colón in Buenos Aires, where winter arrived in July and August, permitting singers to work when Europe's houses were shut for the summer. Just as Paris set the tone for fashion and retailing, Milan ruled the opera stages of the world—no light matter in a period when opening night at the Met was the leading event of the New York season, and divas had the status of today's pop stars and were covered with diamonds by the newly rich tycoons of the industrial world.

But Milan, then as now, was a stopping-off point on

the way to the true wonders of Italy. Tourists went from Milan to Venice, stopping at Vicenza, Verona, and Padua on the way. In the eighteenth and nineteenth centuries alike, Palladio's monuments were of particular interest; they had inspired Inigo Jones as they had Thomas Jefferson, who transferred the neoclassical perfection of the Villa Rotonda to his beloved Monticello in Virginia. Padua was visited for its great university, where humanism had reigned in the Renaissance; many young Englishmen settled there for a year or two while attending courses. The great wonder of Padua, Giotto's frescoes at the Scrovegni Chapel, slumbered until the late nineteenth century, since Gothic painting had fallen out of fashion.

VENICE

If given a magical choice of visiting Venice in the comfort of the modern age or the inconvenience and squalor of the seventeenth and eighteenth centuries, any educated tourist would opt for the latter. He would be obliged to risk stabbing by the many bandits who stalked the narrow streets, or being kidnapped by gondoliers who were mixed up in any intrigue, and he would have to put up with the incredible stench and filth of the narrow canals whose accumulated garbage

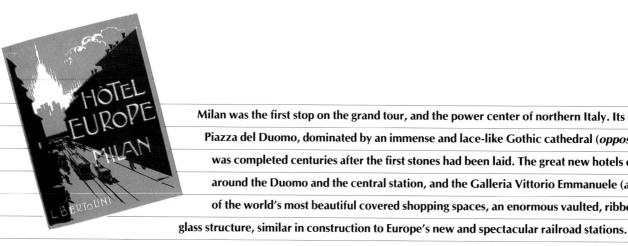

Milan was the first stop on the grand tour, and the power center of northern Italy. Its heart was the Piazza del Duomo, dominated by an immense and lace-like Gothic cathedral (*opposite*) which was completed centuries after the first stones had been laid. The great new hotels clustered around the Duomo and the central station, and the Galleria Vittorio Emmanuele (*above*) was one of the world's most beautiful covered shopping spaces, an enormous vaulted, ribbed steel and glass structure, similar in construction to Europe's new and spectacular railroad stations.

ROME

Rome's most delightful hotel is the d'Inghilterra off the Via Condotti; nearby, on the Piazza di Spagna, is the English Tea Room. They recall the Eternal City's eighteenth-century English coffeehouses and English inns; there was even an English college. The permanent British colony included the pretender Cardinal Duke of York and the Duke of Somerset. There was also a French academy and a German college, but the British—as usual—led the pack. They came to see the ancient sights, to relive Catullus and Julius Caesar, to summon up the agonies of persecuted early Christians. They also came because of the pope and the Vatican's pageantry, although earlier Protestants had to keep clear of the Inquisition. Finally, they came because of the brilliant and rich aristocracy living in great palaces —the Palazzo Borghese, filled with antiquities and Renaissance masterpieces; the Villa Torlonia; the Palazzo Barberini; and the Palazzo Sacchetti.

In the eighteenth century, ancient Rome was largely unexcavated. The poor dwelt in the Theater of Marcellus; the Arch of Severus was hardly visible; and the Colosseum was filled with sheds for animals. Hubert Robert's scenes of laundry hanging from splendid arches and pretty girls languishing on the debris of the Roman Empire are quite accurate representations of the contemporary scene. They were bought as souvenirs, as were works by Panini and Piranesi, and English aristocrats had their portraits painted by Pompeo Batoni, who always filled the background with the architecture of the Eternal City.

A generation of archaeologists led by Winckelmann

This view of Florence by A. Marks, painted most probably from the Piazzale Michelangelo, shows the

magnificent Renaissance city through which the Arno flows in timeless serenity. Florence was a place for

contemplation and study, a magnet for philosophers, art collectors and writers. It never had the frivolity and

madness of the other cities and resorts of Europe. Florence has always been noted for its cleanliness, sobriety

and conservatism, and its aristocratic ladies ran finishing schools for upper-class European and American girls

who were trained to discuss the classical past on appropriate occasions.

finally uncovered the ancient splendors for nineteenth-century visitors, who now found that Rome had become a royal capital. The House of Savoy ruled a united Italy from the Quirinale beginning in 1870, bringing visiting monarchs in its wake. This court paralleled the Vatican's pomp, splitting the aristocracy into two factions—the black supporting the pope and the white the king.

The kings of Italy were new to their trade, with households not equipped for visiting monarchs and their suites. As usual, César Ritz came to the rescue with the Grand Hotel, modeled after his other European successes. English plumbers and French upholsterers soon arrived, the suites of rooms all had their private baths. Escoffier directed the kitchens and on January 17, 1893 Prince Colonna, the mayor of Rome, hailed Ritz as "the new César, returned to conquer Rome." It was for the Grand Hotel that Ritz

The Colosseum (*left*) and the Arch of Constantine (*right*) photographed at the beginning of the century. These two monuments near the Forum Romanum were but two of many recently restored sites that drew visitors to Rome. The Forum itself had been the commercial, administrative and judicial center of the Empire, a site of marvelous colonnaded basilicas and other public buildings started by Julius Caesar and carried on by his nephew, the Emperor Augustus. At its completion, the Forum was filled with statuary, gilded bronze, columns and priceless marble, and perfectly mirrored the prestige and power of the Roman Empire. After the decline of the Empire, all this was pillaged and the Forum was buried in rubbish until the nineteenth-century revival of interest in antiquity inspired new excavations.

invented indirect lighting, putting bulbs between plates of frosted glass, in ceiling moldings and alabaster urns. And Rome was now to have *its* "season" from December to April as an alternative to the Cote d'Azur or the Nile. In the fashion of the Belle Epoque, Ritz organized cotillions, balls and entertainments for his international clientele (not yet called the jet set), bringing the secluded Roman princes and princesses out of their dark Renaissance and Baroque piles into the pink candle-light of his dining and ballrooms. The Pope didn't approve, but Rome had a new dimension. It was Michelangelo's "Last Judgment" in the afternoon and Proust's "Swann's Way" in the evening.

The Colosseum, originally called the Amphiteatrum Flavium, was completed by Titus in 80 A.D. and was the largest theater in the world seating 40–50,000 spectators in an elliptical space whose circumference was nearly a third of a mile. It was inaugurated by gladiatorial combats lasting 100 days in which 5,000 wild animals were killed, and it of course witnessed the martyrdom of many Christians. There was no monument in ancient Rome which so vividly accented for visitors the life of the ancient capital. The Arch of Constantine was the best preserved of the many triumphal arches in Rome.

NAPLES AND SOUTH

It is difficult today to imagine the attraction southern Italy held for travellers from the seventeenth century up until World War I. The development of the great trains, ocean liners and later the airplane brought new destinations to the timetables of such great agencies as Thomas Cook. As we shall see later, Egypt and India were the first to enter the repertory as places to seek the sun in winter. Spain came next, as did Portugal, when CIWL inaugurated an express from Saint Petersburg right through to Lisbon, despite the complications of changing bogies to fit the different tracks of the Iberian Peninsula. For rich Americans, Henry Flagler developed the magnificent resorts of Florida starting with the Ponce de Leon in St. Augustine, going on to the Royal Poinciana and Breakers in Palm Beach and ending with Miami, although he had his eye on Havana. For the Grand Tourist of the seventeenth and eighteenth centuries, winter sun was found in Naples; Sicily came into the picture in the nineteenth century thanks to better roads, boats, trains and hotels. Catania and Siracusa were, for many years, Europe's Palm Beach, with a Spring-like climate from December to March and wonderful excursions to the well preserved temples in Segesta, Selinunte and Paestum.

Naples and Sicily shared a Bourbon king, who reigned from his magnificent palace at Caserta, built to rival Versailles, and Naples had a rich and amusing aristocracy that had the means to entertain on a grand scale. In the eighteenth century, it was the biggest city in Italy, the third-largest metropolis in Europe, and boasted San Carlo, one of the most beautiful opera houses in the world. Its bay was clean and beautiful, studded with volcanoes that performed day and night for enchanted tourists, lighting up the skies and reflecting fire on the waters. After the unification of Italy under one royal family, the Bourbons ceased to rule and Naples lost much of its glamour. The Industrial Revolution was welcomed in northern Italy, but alien to the fun-loving society of the south, which rapidly created a schism between northern and southern Italy that still exists today.

Naples became one of the first victims of urban squalor and poverty, beggars and thieves roamed its streets at a time when they were being controlled in other great European cities, and this delightful former capital of a rich state became a stopping-off place on the way to Capri, Sorrento, Amalfi, Pompeii, and

Above A view of Naples—the beach at Marinella with the castle of St Elmo in the background. The streets of Naples, the most populous city in Italy, swarmed with life: people cooked on the pavement with the hawkers, pickpockets, food-sellers and naked children around them. It was scarcely surprising that cholera was endemic. The fishermen sold their catch to street-kitchens around the port.

Vesuvius seen from Posillipo by Wright of Derby (1734–1797). This beautiful example of British romantic painting shows the great volcano erupting during the full moon, its flames reflected on the calm waters of the Bay of Naples. Posillipo was one of the hills of Naples from which were enjoyed the best views of Vesuvius and the Bay of Naples. This is typical of the pictures painted for the grand eighteenth-century tourist who wanted a souvenir of his European trip. Many English grandees were painted by Pompeo Batoni with Italy's monuments in the background, and Britain's Consul Smith in Venice provided his rich compatriots with masterpieces by Canaletto, Guardi, and other Renaissance and Baroque masters. The richness of the British royal and aristocratic collections is largely a product of the grand tour.

Herculaneum. But still Goethe had written in his *Italienische Reise* "Naples is a Paradise, in it everyone lives in a sort of intoxicated self-forgetfulness. It is just like this with me. I scarcely recognize myself. I feel like a different man."

It was not just the climate. Neapolitans were fun loving and had no inhibitions: stark naked children wandered around bathing on the beaches. The grand Neapolitan palaces were open to suitably born gentlemen and parties went on till dawn. The Prince of Francovilla ended his evenings by making his young lovers jump into the sea, while the Duke of Monte Leone held the most magnificent assembly in town, spending fortunes on ices, other refreshment and decoration.

The young, good looking Neapolitan boys were easily available for gentlemen who preferred them to the 10,000 active courtesans, and buggery became one of the popular pastimes of southern Italy. After the invention of photography, the rich Belgian Baron de Gloeden travelled to Naples and Sicily with his glass plates, photographing pre-pubescent, brown, naked boys posed as ancient statuary with wreaths intertwined in their greasy black hair, and Capri became the *fin de siècle* equivalent of Fire Island or Hamamet under the aegis of expatriate German literati.

In 1775, Robert Adam had seen the beginning of the digging at Herculaneum and ten years later excavations started at Pompeii. For contemporaries brought up on the history of the Roman Empire, these discoveries were of herculean importance. Living cities suddenly put to sleep by a rain of deadly ashes and a river of molten lava emerged like Sleeping Beauty from the spiderweb woven by the wicked witch. Walls frescoed with mythological and domestic scenes reappeared in a better state than medieval painting, and patrician houses were dug out untouched by time, their owners still lying where they had fallen nearly two thousand years before. Ruins had been replaced by ancient reality, and suddenly the pretentious Baroque borrowings of the antique vocabulary seemed silly and overblown. There was a return to the pure antique that influenced the decorative arts of Europe in a major way.

Before leaving Naples, the tourist explored Vesuvius itself, climbing over the rocky lava and peering into its smelly sulfurous core. The grand tour of Italy, started on the ice of the Alps, finished appropriately with the flames of a volcano.

Above A Neapolitan boy photographed by Baron de Gloeden in December 1903. De Gloeden usually photographed pubescent children naked, in classical poses. Young and poor boys in southern Italy lent themselves easily to the vices of tourists from the North and were the counterpoint of the courtesans who worked in the many gambling houses, or *ridotti*, of Venice. Right A poster for the funicular going to Vesuvius: the train belonged to Thomas Cook.

The visit to Vesuvius and Pompeii was an essential part of the grand tour. Pompeii had been a favorite retreat of upper-class Romans who bought houses in the vicinity. An earthquake of 63 A.D. destroyed much of the small city, which was renovated in the style of imperial Rome only to be entombed under a rain of pumice stones, lava and ashes sixteen years later. Although parts of Pompeii were pillaged throughout the centuries, much of it was well preserved by its volcanic burial, particularly many frescoes which were only a few years old at the time of the disaster. The Civic Forum, seen above, was paved with large slabs and embellished with numerous statues, many dedicated to officials of high rank. On one end was the Temple of Jupiter, and the other sides were enclosed by a colonnade.

THE ORIENT EXPRESS

Samples of marqueterie
from CIWL luxury cars.

Prête-moi ton grand bruit, ta grande allure si douce,
Ton glissement nocturne a travers l'Europe illuminée,
O Train de Luxe! Et l'angoissante musique,
Que bruit le long de tes couloirs de cuir doré,
Tandis que derrière les portes laquées, aux loquets de cuivre lourd
Dorment les millionnaires.

Je parcours en chantonnant tes couloirs
Et je suis ta course vers Vienne et Budapest,
Melant ma voix à tes cent mille voix
O Harmonika-Zug!

Valery Larbaud, *Ode*

Lend me your great noise, your grand allure so soft,
Your nightly flit across lit-up Europe,
O Train de Luxe! And the squeaky music,
Which wails along your shiny leather-panelled corridors,
Whilst behind the lacquered doors with heavy brass locks
The millionaires sleep.

Singing, I traverse your corridors
And I follow your run to Vienna and Budapest,
Blending my voice to your hundred thousand voices,
O Harmonica Train!

The most glamorous train ever to ride the tracks was the Orient Express. There were several versions of it on various routes, and its service ended after World War II (the current revivals are mere excuses for nostalgia and conspicuous consumption); the train was mourned by both the passengers it had carried and those who never had the chance to enjoy it. Its legend stemmed from a blend of several ingredients:

• It crossed through an extraordinary patchwork of countries and peoples that have, to all effects and purposes, disappeared. The Iron Curtain came down in Vienna at the end of World War II and since then travel in Central Europe has been difficult and sporadic. Also, the character of such countries as Romania, Bulgaria, and Hungary has radically changed; a colorful peasantry, upper class and aristocracy has been eliminated and the standard of living in the region has severely declined.

• Its ultimate destination, Istanbul, was a place of mystery and beauty ruled in the early years of the Express by the last of the Ottoman sultans.

• The itinerary of the Express was fraught with danger. Bandits held up the train and kept its passengers hostage in 1891, it was lost for several days in 1929 in a snow drift near the Turkish border when its passengers could easily have died of exposure or hunger, and the Balkan powder keg was so mercurial that there always the risk of war or revolution.

• Because of its itinerary, the Express carried the most unusual and cosmopolitan passengers. There were royals from the Balkan kingdoms on their way to Europe, maharajas who had come from India by boat to Istanbul in order to take the Express to Paris, diplomatic couriers with a briefcase attached to their wrist, famous musicians, stars of the stage and screen and fading night club dancers on the way to oblivion in the flesh pots of the near East. There were also titans of finance and industry on their way to exploit the fabulous riches of Romania's oil fields or to sell armaments to the litigious Balkan kings.

The Orient Express sleeping car as used on the 1883 maiden voyage for the press. *Left to right* Night position for four passengers, the lavatory at the end of the car, and the day position of the compartment with the upper berths folded back and the lower berths transformed into sofas. The upper berths, in fact, seem to have disappeared totally and it is difficult to work out where they have gone!

A poster for the Orient Express, emphasizing the exotic. Istanbul was, in fact, an oriental city which greatly fascinated Europeans. It was filled with wily traders such as Calouste Gulbenkian (*inset*), who made a fortune as a middleman in the rapidly expanding oil business.

SHADY CHARACTERS

The Orient Express was immortalized in endless books and films; mystery writers were inspired by its rich and shady passengers. Agatha Christie's *Murder on the Orient Express* was set in a snowstorm, inspired by the 1929 incident. There were Maurice Dekobra's *The Madonna of the Sleeping Car* and Graham Greene's *Stamboul Train*. James Bond was put aboard by Ian Fleming, D. H. Lawrence booked a voyage on it for Lady Chatterley and her father, and it also inspired Paul Morand, Eric Ambler, and Alfred Hitchcock.

The most famous and devoted passengers were Calouste Gulbenkian and Basil Zaharoff, two Middle Easterners of doubtful credentials. Gulbenkian, known as Mr. Five Percent, often said that the luxury of the Orient Express and the wealth of its passengers were what inspired him to get rich, which he did by taking a cut on most of the oil that was pumped in the Near East. Zaharoff, "The Merchant of Death," was said to have earned a little over one pound in gold for every

casualty in World War I from the armaments he had sold to both sides. He met the woman of his life in 1886 on the Orient Express, when she fled into his compartment (No. 7) from her mad, aristocratic husband, Don Francisco Principe de Borbon y Borbon, who had just attempted to kill her. No wonder he

Above An assemblage of CIWL personnel in 1914. The brown uniforms varied little throughout Europe, and

the servants seemed able to speak all languages simultaneously. *Below* Hercule Poirot, investigator

extraordinary, walks beside the Orient Express in Sidney Lumet's movie *Murder on the Orient Express* based

on Agatha Christie's novel.

always booked No. 7—and ordered his ashes to be scattered from its window.

In its heyday, when the great express train crossed through the Balkans, peasants never failed to stop to peer through the windows of its blue cars at people from another universe living in conditions of luxury almost beyond their comprehension. Traveling on the Orient Express was a symbol of success, and understandably so. At the time of its maiden voyage, the price of a round-trip ticket from London to Istanbul equaled the annual rent for an elegant London town house, and a servant could come along for fifteen pounds, close to his annual salary. There have been extraordinary developments in travel since the train's first trip in 1883, but the standards of comfort, care, and sheer elegance of the Orient Express have never been surpassed.

THE MAIDEN VOYAGE

Before putting his great express on the tracks, Georges Nagelmackers had to negotiate rights of way with railroads in France, Alsace-Lorraine, Württemberg, the Duchy of Baden, Bavaria, Austria, and Romania, all of which perceived the venture as a threat to their monopolies. He succeeded with the help of his original sponsor and shareholder, King Leopold II of Belgium, who pressured the railway owners through his many royal relatives. The through route to Istanbul was in fact not a reality, since segments of track were incomplete,and the maiden voyage was a combination of a luxury train to the Bulgarian border, a short ferry ride across the Danube, a messy Bulgarian train to the Black Sea and then an overnight ferry to Constantinople.

That first voyage, in 1883, was documented by two famous journalists, Edmond About and the more extravagant Henri Opper de Blowitz. About, an Alsatian, was a sort of latter-day French Trollope or Thackeray, and the trip inspired his book, *De Pontoise à Stamboul*, which is the official version of the first voyage. De Blowitz, a native of Bohemia, was the Paris correspondent for *The Times* of London. He was one of the most famous journalists of his era, and his

pieces were syndicated throughout the world. His presence guaranteed that every hour of the trip would be read about by millions in several languages. De Blowitz also used the trip to get an interview with the King of Romania and the far more inaccessible Sultan of the Ottoman Empire. There were three German journalists, and the literary world was also represented by the young Leon Daudet, whose famous father Alphonse had refused Nagelmackers's invitation. Leon, a vile character, was one of the more virulent accusers of Captain Dreyfus, founded the anti-Semitic journal "Action Francaise" and was an active *collaborateur* during the war. He might be considered the first of a legion of nasties carried on the great train.

The train consisted of a locomotive and tender, a

mail car, two wagon-lit sleeping cars accommodating twenty passengers each, a restaurant car, and a car for baggage and the food, wines, liqueurs, and other luxuries required for the express's high standards. The choice of locomotive was a serious matter: a breakdown in the Balkans would have been disastrous. The train had the latest Westinghouse compressed-air braking system. (In later years, the train's brakes failed once: in 1901, astonished diners in the Frankfurt Hauptbahnhof's buffet recoiled in terror as the giant black locomotive came hurtling toward them. Nobody was hurt, but we must assume that many a bratwurst was left unconsumed.)

The Simplon Orient Express at Milan, 1929–30. This offshoot of

the first Orient Express crossed through Switzerland, the Simplon

Tunnel, and northern Italy on the way to the Balkans or Istanbul.

The service became essential when the Germans, embittered by

reparations payments, created all sorts of impediments to prevent

the express crossing over their tracks.

The sleeping cars were sheathed in teak and mahogany with inlaid marqueterie, the sofa beds covered in gold-tooled cordoba leather. The windows, fitted so carefully that no draft could penetrate them, were embellished with damask drapes tied with gold-tasseled silk cords. Paris was the great innovator of passementerie, the grace notes to upholstery and curtains that were used ad nauseum by the Belle Epoque decorators, and Nagelmackers provided them in profusion. Following Pullman's innovation, the seats turned into beds at night; the delighted passenger found silk sheets, British wool blankets, and a fluffy eiderdown for his or her comfort. It was only later that compartments had their own bathrooms (one could say the same of European and American grand hotels), so passengers had to repair to the end of the car where they found a bathroom with a toilet of Italian marble and a decorated porcelain sink. In a day when sanitation was at a premium, there were clean towels, perfumed soap, crystal flacons of eau de cologne, and a vase of fresh flowers; the porter cleaned the room after every use. The cars were heavily carpeted, well heated, insulated against noise, and cushioned from the irregularities of the track. A delighted de Blowitz remarked on the first morning that he had shaved without cutting himself. Few twentieth-century train passengers can make this claim as they emerge from their night trains covered with Band-Aids.

Following the custom of the times, the dining car had separate salons for ladies and gentlemen. The ladies' was furnished with reproduction Louis XV chairs and delicate *petites tables*; its walls were covered with eighteenth-century tapestries. The gents' saloon had leather chairs and a bookcase to re-create the atmosphere of a London club. At the time, French society had been seized with a sort of anglomania, personified in the Jockey Club, and Nagelmackers made sure his rich male passengers traveled in the style of the day.

At meal times, passengers were summoned by the porter's silver bell or a discreet knock: "*Messieurs, dames—Le diner est servi.*" At the center of the car was the miraculous Wagon Restaurant, subtly lit by large gas chandeliers of brass and crystal. The ceiling was painted with figures from Greek mythology and cherubs by students of the Académie des Beaux-Arts, and the table had little gold-framed original drawings by Delacroix, Schwind, and other artists. Tables for two lined one wall, and four diners were accommodated opposite. Liveried waiters recruited from luxury hotels circulated between the rows of tables, which were set with Baccarat crystal, starched napery, and monogrammed porcelain. The waiters were not allowed to wear glasses, and their anonymity was increased by powdered wigs. (Later, when passengers complained that the powder fell into their soup, the CIWL relented, but without wigs the waiters looked surprisingly odd.) At one end of the car there was a tiny kitchen run by a bearded Burgundian chef, whose six helpers were often scalded when the train gave a sudden lurch.

LEAVING PARIS

This magnificent hotel on wheels awaited its passengers at Paris's Gare de l'Est on October 4, 1883. Nagelmackers had a dilapidated assemblage of rusting Mann boudoir cars parked on the other side of the platform; it was his revenge on his hated ex-partner. Electricity lit the platform and was in the air as the

Above Smoking salon of a CIWL restaurant car around 1900. There is a frescoed ceiling, and the French windows at the end of the car opened onto an observation platform. *Opposite above left* An R-class standard teak CIWL sleeping car, with a washroom shared by two adjoining compartments. *Opposite above right* A compartment of approximately the same date with its own washbasin. Seldom has the beauty of train compartments been equaled in terms of rich and varied marqueterie, luxurious upholstery covered in pressed velvet, extensive use of stained glass, subtle lighting and rich, heavy carpeting. *Below* A CIWL dining car, *c.*1900, used on central European Expresses. The high quality of linen, crystal and crockery indicate the lavishness of both food and service.

chosen few made their way toward "The Magic Carpet to the Orient." Nagelmackers himself was the tour director. There were nineteen representatives of French ministries, banks, and railroad companies; the Ottoman sultan was represented by his Paris chargé d'affaires, Mishak Effendi. The ladies' salon was unused until Vienna, where the trip's only two women boarded: the economical Nagelmackers was not wasting many berths on spouses.

The huge locomotive pulled out of the station with such velvety ease that the passengers hardly realized it. At 8:00 P.M. the first meal was served—ten courses, all and only the best. Over caviar, oysters, lobster, game, vintage wines, Napoleon brandy, and Havana cigars, the powerful gentlemen began cutting deals as the luxurious express swept along. Strasbourg was reached before dawn. A small group of German officials was on the platform to greet the train, but few passengers bothered to rise, preferring the comfort of their warm beds. Herr Porges, the European head of the American Edison Company, lost the opportunity to show the slumbering passengers the station's generator, and to get a few orders in the process.

The train continued through Karlsruhe, Ulm, and Munich to Vienna. As the sun rose, the passengers opened the heavy blinds and damask drapes to watch German peasants harvesting their crops in the crisp autumn morning. The only mishap so far had been in the dining car, where an overheated axle box might have set the extravaganza on fire; but the resourceful Nagelmackers had a substitute car waiting in Munich, and the train proceeded on schedule.

The express crossed into Austria-Hungary at Simbach and arrived in Vienna late in the evening. It was met by a grand reception committee in full dress uniform, headed by Emperor Franz Josef's Court Chamberlain. There were endless speeches, and the band of the Imperial Guard played the hastily learned national anthems of all the countries on the train's route. A rendition of "The Blue Danube" was better, and finally the weary passengers were taken to the flower-filled station restaurant for supper, champagne, and imperial Tokay. Most passengers staggered back to their compartments, but several boarded state carriages to see the newly lit Ringstrasse, the floodlit Opera House, the Hofburg, and the House of Parliament. Finally, an international exhibition of electric lighting had been especially kept open for them. Presumably, Herr Porges had relayed a message to his Viennese colleagues.

Above A ticket folder of 1930 with a map of the Simplon Orient and Taurus Express. As can be seen, cars of the Taurus Express branched off to the Near East, and this folder once contained tickets from London to Tel Kotchek via Baghdad. The Taurus Express connected three times a week with Syria, Palestine and Egypt, twice a week with Iraq and Iran, and weekly with India. *Below* The CIWL staff lines up on the platform at Baydarpasa Station in Istanbul to say goodbye to their clients in 1949. *Opposite* The menu of January 4, 1898 celebrated the 25th anniversary of the founding of the company.

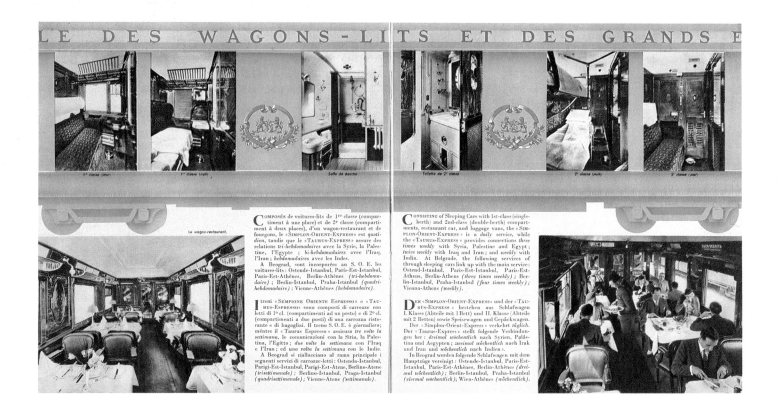

LE DES WAGONS-LITS ET DES GRANDS E

KAISER·FRANZ·JOSEF·PLATZ

Above A brochure for the Simplon Orient Express and the Taurus Express showing

the comfortable accommodations. There seems to be little difference between the

first- and second-class sleeping arrangements except for the installation of an

upstairs bunk. *Below* One of Otto Wagner's designs for the new Vienna.

Undoubtedly the principal influence on the regeneration of Vienna at the turn of

the century, his work carefully integrates the magnificent existing buildings.

HALTESTELLE · WESTBAHNHOF.

Vienna was a major stop on the route of the Orient Express. *Above* The new Ring whose centerpiece was the opera house. *Below* More architectural drawings by Otto Wagner. Baroness Eugénie de Rothschild (*inset*) was one of the doyennes of Vienna society in the 1930s.

VIENNA

Vienna at the end of the century was not only among the grandest of European capitals, it was a place of incredible cultural, intellectual and social life, the center of a wide-flung monarchy whose power was fully expressed in the building program of the Ring. The Ringstrasse, built in the 1860s as Vienna's answer to Haussmann's Paris boulevards, was conceived as a thoroughfare for the rapid movement of troops. It inspired many important buildings designed eclectically in what came to be known as the Ringstrasse style: the classical Greek Parliament, the Gothic City Hall, the Italian Renaissance university and twin museums of art history and natural history, and the French Renaissance new Court Opera.

The Opera, finished in 1869, was the center of the new Vienna, and the city's best hotels—Sacher's, Bristol's, and the Imperial—sprouted up around it. It was run with an iron hand by Gustav Mahler, and had in its pit the legendary Vienna Philharmonic. Verdi conducted there, and Wagner stayed at the Imperial. Richard Strauss was shortly to come on the scene with his bittersweet *Der Rosenkavalier*, and Johann Strauss conducted his waltzes every year at the Opera Ball. The highlight of Vienna's season, the ball was attended by the emperor and the aristocratic families of the city. (Strauss could always be found running from restaurant to ballroom; he could collect a higher fee if he put in a personal appearance.)

Waltzing was the rage in Vienna. The great families

Above **A view of the Prater, Vienna's famous pleasure park. Situated close to Leopoldstadt, the Jewish quarter, it was, at the end of the last century, the favorite leisure attraction of the city.**

of the empire all had palaces in Vienna, as did the newly rich bankers, and the season for the Liechtensteins, Lobkowiczes, Schönbrunns, Esterhazys, and, more recently, Rothschilds was an endless suite of balls, musicales, and court dinners. The usual contingent of Russian grand dukes and other continental grandees arrived on the express trains and stayed in the new hotels. The action was at Sacher's, just behind the Opera, particularly in the many *chambres priveés*, where gossip, intrigue, and flirtations flourished. It was the custom to have a late lunch at Sacher's before dining at the Hofburg; the emperor—unlike Edward VII—followed a spartan regime, and his guests had to put down knife and fork as soon as he had cleaned his plate.

There was no end of activities. The new museums displayed exceptionally rich collections and the Hofburg could be visited during special hours, as could the splendid gardens and palace at Schönbrunn, the Hapsburgs' answer to Versailles. The great princely families—Harrach, Liechtenstein, Czernin, and Schönbrunn—also opened their palaces and collections to the public on certain days, and the Albertina had the world's largest collection of old master drawings and prints. Tourists could also go out to the Vienna woods and visit the many *Heurigen* to taste the new wine and picnic in their gardens. And, of course, there was the life of the coffeehouse, without which Vienna would have sunk into despair. The first of these had been founded near Saint Stephen's Cathedral in the eighteenth century, and the institution quickly became a place to meet friends, make

Above The fashionable Viennese parade down the Hauptalle in dignified carriages and racy new automobiles on their way to the many restaurants and cafés of the Prater.

contacts, read the newspapers, play chess, argue, and plot revolutions and upheavals, all for the price of a *kleine Brauner* or a *Melange*. Intellectuals frequented the Café Griensteid —nicknamed Café Megalomania by its clients. It was replaced at century's end by the Café Central, where Trotsky and Lenin were regulars. Franz Lehar and other musicians preferred the Café Speal, while Stefan Zweig, Arthur Schnitzler, Egon Schiele, Sigmund Freud, Gustav Klimt, and Adolf Loos could be found at all hours at other smoke-filled cafés.

TO BUDAPEST

Nagelmackers' passengers had no time for a coffee on their tour of Vienna. The train had to continue its long journey and the passenger list had now been aug-

mented by Herr von Scala, Austria's Vice-Minister of Roads and Communications, his wife and sister-in-law Mme Leonie Pohl, the only ladies on the inaugural trip. The short distance from Vienna to Budapest, a mere 150 miles, was covered during the night, and early in the morning the train reached Budapest traveling at very slow speed so that its passengers could enjoy the sights. Along the Danube, the train moved between the two hills dominating Buda, an ancient town then imbued with the Oriental atmosphere left behind by Tatar, Mongol, and Turkish invaders. The Gellert Hill rose from the river and was crowned with a military citadel; beyond was Castle Hill with a neo-baroque palace built by the Empress Maria Theresa and now being transformed into a gigantic Hapsburg residence. On the east side of the Danube was Pest (Budapest was created in 1871 by linking Buda, Pest, and the old Roman city of Obuda). Pest was modern, centrally planned, and in an early state of growth. At the station, a military band played czardas, and steaming kettles of goulash fed the passengers, who were not allowed to leave the station.

GYPSIES

At Szegedin, an ancient city, Nagelmackers gave his passengers a delightful surprise—a gypsy band dressed in traditional silks and golden jewelry. In the dining car they sang and played for two solid hours until the

Above The vestibule, main salon and grill room of the Hotel Astoria in Budapest clearly demonstrates the luxury of the Austro-Hungarian capital. *Below* The Cook's office in Zagreb. A gypsy (*inset*), one of thousands who wandered around central Europe, singing in night clubs, conjuring, acting in circuses or telling fortunes. *Opposite* A poster for Hungary's millennium, by Theo van Rysselberghe, illustrates the glories of the country's capital. *Below* The Franz Josef Bridge over the Danube connecting the two cities of Buda and Pest.

train reached Temesvar (now Timisoara), in Romania. The swarthy band leader introduced himself as Onody Kahniar, king of the gypsies, and soon the two ladies who had boarded in Vienna were invited to dance. The Burgundian chef asked the gypsy king to play "La Marseillaise," and there was not a dry eye as the passengers joined in.

Before World War II gypsies were encountered from Vienna to Istanbul; many were annihilated in Hitler's concentration camps or assimilated into European civilization. There are, of course, some gypsies still with us, particularly in Southern Spain where they were out of reach of the Nazis, but this fascinating tribe has become an oddity rather than a vital force whose talented people spread their rich folklore from India to Saint Petersburg. Particularly dominant in Central Europe, gypsies traced their origin to Northern India; their seemingly non-ending and improvised songs enriched the music of Kodaly as well as Franz Liszt. They were great tourist attractions, although they had to make a living by begging, telling fortunes, stealing, singing and doing odd jobs as their perpetual wandering deprived them of steady work. As a minority, they were excluded from peasant life, and as non-conformists they could never settle down.

Nagelmackers had pulled off a brilliant stunt by inviting the band aboard and, after the gypsy musicians had left, the train rolled across the *puszta*,

or Hungarian plain, toward the Transylvanian Alps. Nagelmackers and his distinguished guests had reached the land of Count Dracula.

ROMANIA

In 1883, Romania was a country with immense potential. Its rich, black soil was heavily planted with sun flowers and wheat. The neat, clean villages had charming stone or wooden churches; many of them were gaily painted inside and out from the Middle Ages. The peasants, beautifully dressed in costumes that varied from village to village, kept droves of elephant-colored Nilotic cattle and herds of sheep. And Romania was studded with rich oil fields. The country was ruled by King Carol, a Hohenzollern prince, and his mystic wife, Queen Elizabeth, better known as Carmen Sylva, who was also a poet. They had invited the passengers to their new Castle Peles in the resort of Sinaia, eighty-five miles from Bucharest.

En route, the train passed the Danube's spectacular Iron Gates, a natural phenomenon formed by massive boulders emerging from the waters. The track was unsteady; storms had eroded the subsoil, and the train's engineer watched carefully for avalanche debris on the tracks. At Bucharest the train was shunted to a junction for the short trip past oil derricks, forests, and streams to Sinaia. The castle, a Germanic, turreted pile on a hill among splendid mountains, resembled Saint Moritz's Palace Hotel. The party was first taken to the Grand Hotel Nouls, where they lunched on delicious white caviar and local crayfish and were serenaded by a gypsy band. Had they not been quickly summoned by an officer from the Court, they could have crossed the street for a delicious pastry at the renowned Confiserie Kalinzachis, whose speciality was a tart made with wild raspberries so delicious that the Carpathian bears were willing to risk life and limb to gather them up into their soft paws.

The passengers were led into the courtyard, past the entrance hall into the Hall of Honor where they found King Carol dressed in parade uniform complete with a

---

Above **The Athenée Palace in Bucharest.** *Opposite* **The Timosiana branch of CIWL. The Athenee Palace**

was *the* grand hotel of the Romanian capital, the center of a country then rich from oil and agriculture.

A strange mixture of East and West, of rich and poor, Bucharest enjoyed a lively social life dominated

by an intrigue-filled court and idle aristocracy. The city's great boulevards were filled with fine

restaurants and elegant shops, and the size of the "Birou de Voiaj" indicates that there was lots of

money available for travel even in distant parts of the country.

BIROU DE VOIAJ

COMPAGNIE INTERNATIONALE
DES
WAGONS-LITS
ET DES GRANDS EXPRESS EUROPÉENS
AGENTIA TIMISOARA
WAGONS LITS-WAGONS RESTAURANTS
TRAINS DE LUXE-TRAINS BLEUS

BILETE **C.F.R.** INTERNATIONALE
PENTRU TOATE DESTINATII CLASA I II III
SERVICIUL MARITIM ROMÂN
BILETE DE **VAPOARE**
ASIGURAREA BAGAGELOR
VIZE DE **PASAPOARTE**
PROSPECTE SI INFORMATIUNI GRATUITE

ENTRÉE

tall plumed hat with heavy gold tassels. Carmen Sylva, his Queen, was wrapped in a Romanian national costume and the courtiers wore tails or uniform, putting the bedraggled passengers to shame. The group was given a tour of the hideous palace and then attended a concert by the famous Romanian soprano, Carlotta Leria, badly accompanied by the Queen, while de Blowitz interviewed the King about the state of the Balkans. The visit was at an end, the party walked down the hill in the rain, got back into the train and reached Bucharest at 10:00 that night.

BUCHAREST

Romania's capital, known as "little Paris," was inhabited by a mix of gypsies, Armenian merchants, Turks, Phanariot Greeks, Sephardic Jews, Russians, and, of course, Romanians. It was so hot in the summer that everything stopped from noon until 5:00, and so cold in the winter that life seemed to come to a total halt. Its two main boulevards, the Soseaua Kiseleff and the Calea Victoriei, were beautiful, tree-lined facades hiding incredible hovels. Rich and poor lived side by side in Bucharest, which had become the capital just two years before.

As for the rich, the weekly gala at the opera was followed by balls and supper parties in large, Parisianstyle town houses. People went about in carriages drawn by pairs of valuable black Orloffs and driven by Russian *izvoschiki*. The drivers belonged to a strange sect, the Skoptsi, who believed Christ still lived, a celibate wandering the earth in various forms (in emulation, they had themselves emasculated after fathering one child).

The Nagelmackers party dined in one of the capital's renowned garden restaurants, known as *gradina*, which filled only after midnight and often featured gypsy and Russian orchestras. Romanian cuisine was delicious; a dinner could consist of *ciorbă*, a fish or chicken soup made with sour cream, followed by carp, perch, or sturgeon (Romania's caviar was as fine as Russia's or Persia's). Other specialties, reflecting

Turkish influence, were *dolmas* (stuffed grape leaves), *sarmăla* (rice balls with chopped meat), and *ardeĭ umplatĭ* (paprika pods with rice and ground meat). And, finally, Romanian women were renowned for their beauty and sexual invention; but at this point Edmond About's detailed account of the Orient Express's Bucharest stopover is regrettably short of detail.

THE END OF THE LINE

Long after midnight, the express departed for the small frontier port of Giurgiu. On the other side of the Danube was Ruschuk in Bulgaria, and the passengers were forced to trade their lovely train for a primitive ferry. After the crossing, they boarded a far less comfortable train that took them to the Bulgarian town of Varna on the Black Sea. Bulgaria was an appallingly chaotic country ruled by another German princeling, Alexander of Battenberg, who had been placed on his throne by Queen Victoria and the czar of Russia.

Above The Therapia Palace was one of the grandest hotels on the banks of the Bosporus, popular not only with Turkish nobles and dignitaries from the Ottoman Empire, but also with visitors from Europe and the United States.

Bandits had just burned the station at Vatova, through which the train would pass, and passengers took out their pistols in fear of an attack. There was none, but on May 31, 1891, there was a holdup in Cherkes Keri in East Thrace; hostages were taken and a giant ransom paid. The bandit leader, styling himself "Anasthatos, Leader of Rebels," ordered the passengers around in three languages and more than $1,000,000 (in today's terms) was stolen. De Blowitz and About had to settle for describing the miserable countryside and its bullet-riddled houses, and grumbled about the poor food. They had nothing good to say about Varna, where passengers embarked on the *Espero*, the run-down ferry that was to take them to Constantinople.

THE GOLDEN HORN

Dawn broke as the *Espero* entered the Bosporus and pointed her bow toward Istanbul. Today, Istanbul is a dilapidated city in a somewhat backward country; in 1883, Orient Express passengers could still see the last glory of the Ottoman sultans who had once ruled large parts of the world, from Greece and the Balkans to as far as the gates of Vienna, up to most of what is today called the Middle East and Egypt (but for Prince Eugene of Savoy in the siege of 1683, they might have ruled Austria as well). If the Turks did not capture Europe, they did capture the European imagination, influencing painting, decoration, and theater. Whenever an exotic, funny, powerful, or mysterious role had to be filled in an eighteenth-century opera, a sultan or a janissary was hauled in; when a victim was needed, there would be a beautiful harem slave. Nineteenth-century painting is unimaginable without odalisques, eunuchs, sultans, and sultanas. *Turquerie* became an obsession, and that explains the quickened heartbeat of Nagel-mackers' friends as they came down the channel with the magnificent Palace of Dolmabahçe on the one bank and the Beylerbey Palace on the other. The blue Mediterranean sparkled in the early sun; an armada of small and large ships rode the waters; and in the distance rose the minarets and domes of Haghia Sophia and the Blue Mosque.

Above **A view of the Dolmabahçe Palace, which replaced Topkapi**

as the residence of the Ottoman sultan at the end of the

nineteenth century.

Waiting on the pier were the Belgian ambassador; Sheker Pasha, the sultan's chamberlain; and other Turkish officials in tail coats and fezzes. The intrepid passengers proceeded by carriage to the Pera Palace Hotel, the newest and most luxurious in the city. They saw the Topkapi, an astonishing series of fortified buildings from which the Ottomans had ruled the world by *firman*, and were dazzled by its collections of Korans and jewel-encrusted swords and daggers. The Topkapi also had a fabulous collection of Oriental miniatures and a warehouse filled with priceless Chinese porcelain. Watching the group through filigreed stone windows were the last of the harem ladies, still protected by their fat, beardless eunuchs with high-pitched voices.

At the Beylerbey Palace, where Empress Eugénie had stayed, the passengers were entertained by belly dancers, and later they drove through the Dolma Valley to the Yildiz Kiosk, where the Sultan Abdul Hamid lived in secluded luxury with his wives and court dwarf. The self-styled "Emperor of Powerful Emperors, the Sole Arbiter of the World's Destiny; Refuge of Sovereigns; Distributor of Crowns to the Kings of the World; Ruler of Europe, Asia, and Africa; High King of the Two Seas; Shadow of Allah upon the Earth," Abdul Hamid in fact was ever in sheer terror of being bumped off. He had killed several close members of his family, murdered many of his ministers, generals, and other court officials, and was responsible for the genocide of the Armenians. Gladstone called him the Great Assassin, and he was otherwise known as Abdul the Damned. As his covered carriage was carried to a platform from which he inspected his troops, the Orient Express group watched in fascination—all save de Blowitz, who arranged another interview for the front page of newspapers around the world.

Like all good tour directors, Nagelmackers gave his charges time to shop in the bazaar, lunch in the open-air restaurants along the Bosporus, watch the devoted Muslims called to prayer from the minarets, and even go to the famous *hammams*, where they were steamed, massaged, scraped, bathed, and cooled as they drank sweet rose water or mint tea. Refreshed and rested, they then repaired to the pier to begin the return trip to Paris along the same route by which they had come. They arrived at the Gare de l'Est at 6:00 P.M., on schedule, eleven days after embarking on a journey that would become part of travel folklore. Jules Verne went around the world in eighty days, but Nagelmackers' achievement was a reality.

LOCOMOTIVES AND KINGS

The Orient Express was scheduled to leave Paris on Tuesdays and Fridays and return from Istanbul on Wednesdays and Saturdays. The full route took eighty-one hours and forty minutes, but the much shorter Paris–Vienna trip was the most popular (beginning in 1885, the train included cars for only that portion, and on three nights a week there was an abridged Orient Express that simply ran between the two capitals). When track was laid between Bucharest and Constanta, a Romanian Black Sea port, the train could avoid the uncomfortable Danube ferry and the Bulgarian ordeal.

In 1885, the Orient Express ran a weekly service from Budapest to Belgrade and Nis, which forced passengers to take a dreadful horse diligence to Sofia, whence they continued by train to Istanbul. The diligence was run by Brankovits, a ferocious coachman

Above **A suite at the Pera Palace, decorated in the European style.**

Opposite **The bridge over the Bosporus at Galata.**

whose main job was to scare off bandits; needless to say, the sea route was more popular. By 1888, the line through Bulgaria had been finished, and Nagelmackers sent the Vicomte de Richemont to negotiate passage with King Ferdinand. Richemont arrived in Sofia on Brankovits's ghastly diligence; worse, he had no court uniform for his visit, a violation of protocol. Improvising, he borrowed a Bulgarian police captain's uniform, which so amused the king that he immediately signed an agreement. Ferdinand never let the CIWL forget the immense favor he had done them, and after World War I, when he styled himself czar of Bulgaria, he always traveled with his special car attached to the Orient Express free of charge. The problem was that he loved playing engineer, and there was no denying him on his own territory. The engineers did not mind; one even said that he would gladly have given him a job if he were not a king. Ferdinand's son Boris was less

talented, however, and the engineers dreaded the sight of him. He always wore white overalls and was eager to beat the schedule. Once, he forced the fireman to shovel so much coal that the engineer had to blow off steam to prevent an explosion. As it was, the poor fireman was incinerated. (King Ferdinand always said Bulgaria was a ridiculous country!) At any rate, the Orient Express could now go straight through, saving sixteen hours.

Beginning in 1906, the Simplon Orient Express reached Trieste through the Alpine tunnel; it continued through Zagreb and Belgrade to Istanbul after World War I. During the war, the line from Salonika to Larissa had been completed, so cars could now branch off at Belgrade and go all the way to Athens. The embittered Germans made it as difficult as possible for the train to cross their territory, particularly after French and Belgian troops occupied the Ruhr in 1923

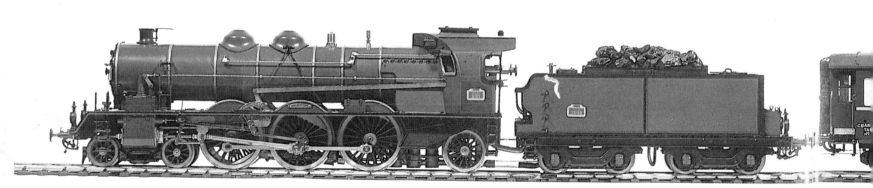

Above **A handsome scale model of**

the Orient Express

as punishment for Germany's not paying its reparations. That is why the Arlberg Orient Express was born, which ran via Switzerland and Austria.

The Orient Express was such an important link between East and West that it had the honor of being the only train written into the peace settlements of the two world wars. Perhaps with Eastern Europe now freed from the Soviet yoke, the train can be revived. If so, it will certainly be fully booked by enthusiasts from all over the world.

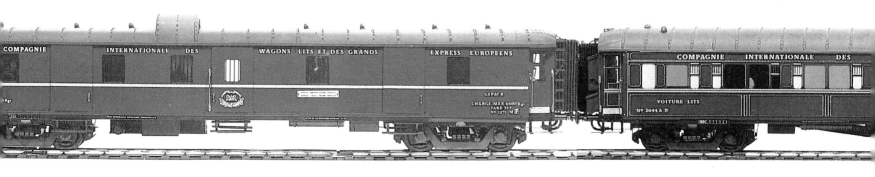

Above **A detail from a**

finely-fashioned piece of

Vuitton luggage.

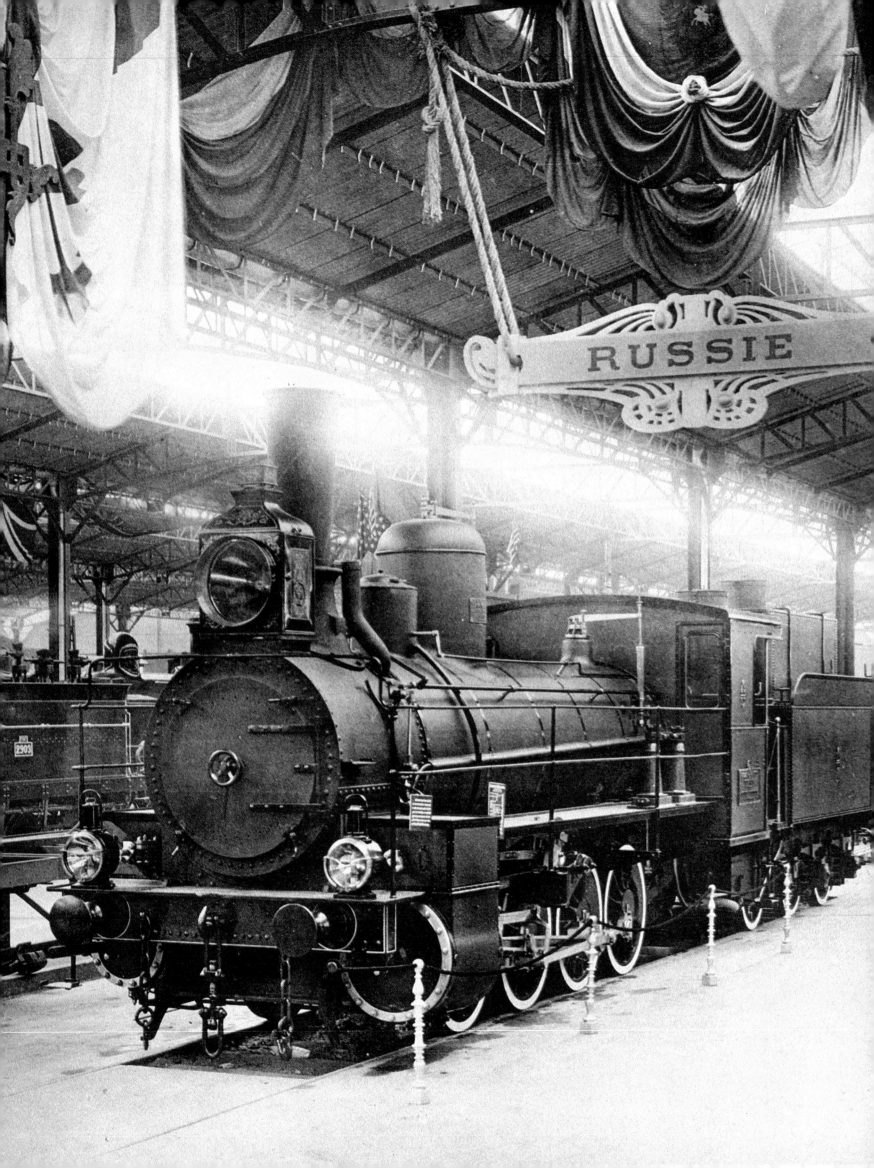

TO RUSSIA AND THE STEPPES

Opposite **The engines and cars for the Trans-Siberian service of**

CIWL were featured in a separate pavilion in the Bois de

Vincennes during the 1900 *Exposition Universelle*.

There was even a dining car from which one could see the

steppes unrolling on a cyclorama while consuming borscht

and beef Stroganov.

Few countries seemed as mysterious as Russia did in the early years of this century. Its seemingly impenetrable land mass stretched from Europe to the Far East, from the Arctic to the deserts and arid mountains where Islam reigned.

Like a schizophrenic, imperial Russia looked East from Moscow, its ancient capital, and West from Saint Petersburg, its intellectual heart. Mongolian peasants and Muslims met Saint Petersburg aristocrats and Moscow businessmen on the great trains and boats that crossed its land mass and mighty lakes and rivers.

Imperial Russia, as the Soviet Union today, was a land where a brilliant intelligentsia was often stifled by a fearful government. Advanced scientific achievement had been paralleled by ignorance, lavish wealth by dire poverty, liberalism by brutal repression. The czar, or "Little Father," ruled over this complex mosaic of peoples, economies, and cultures. Whether in Saint Petersburg or Moscow, he was imagined watching over all his subjects. Hats were doffed in respect to his image, which was in every public place.

A largely corrupt, incompetent, and immutable bureaucracy impeded the progress of this great land that had gone straight from the Middle Ages to modern times without seeing the Renaissance. And yet, what a golden age it was that finally arrived in the nineteenth century, as if a great pool of national genius had been trapped underground to suddenly explode through the

cracks of liberalism. In half a century Russia gave us Tolstoy, Dostoevski, Gogol, and Pushkin; Tchaikovsky, Rimski-Korsakov, Glinka, and Borodin; Stanislavski, Meyerhold, and the modern theater; Pavlova, Nijinsky, and the Ballets Russes. This golden age coincided largely with the Belle Epoque, and it is no wonder that Europe's aristocrats and business tycoons rushed eastward in the great expresses of Georges Nagelmackers, while Russian nobles of uncountable wealth and businessmen of enormous ambition traveled west to spend their fortunes, trade, and make colossal deals. Coinciding with this extraordinary cultural blossoming was a new industrial age in which, surprisingly, ancient Russia was one of the most dynamic participants, surpassing even Great Britain in the development of new industries and factories. And as Moscow drew businessmen and bankers from the entire world, the Saint Petersburg season drew the royal families and aristocracy of Europe to its endless round of balls, receptions, and imperial occasions to which people in precious furs rushed over snow-covered streets in droshkies, whose steaming horses were whipped on by brightly liveried *izvoschiki*.

Rushing along the elegant streets of the imperial capital was easy compared to traveling across Russia's great land mass. Roads were extremely primitive and badly kept, bandits abounded, and the extremes of climate defeated all but the most dedicated traveler. The enormous natural resources of imperial Russia, until the mid-nineteenth century, were carried sporadically along her great rivers, which were frozen over for several months a year and then clogged with melting ice and debris. Caravans also traveled on the *trakts*, or inland routes, which worked better when frozen, since they were reduced to mush in the spring and to sand in the summer. The key to both transport and unlocking Russia's riches lay in the railroad, and the imperial government moved as fast as its cumbersome bureaucracy would permit. The development of the railroads, like much else in imperial Russia, was largely dependent on imperial edict. When Czar Nicholas I decided that it was time to create a railroad between the old and new capitals, he simply took out his ruler and drew a straight line between the two points—and thus the tracks remain today. Anything in the way of the imperial pencil was simply obliterated

None of the superb cars exhibited at the *Exposition* ever reached Russia since the company

wisely wished to avoid ruining its rolling stock on the poorly built track that crossed Siberia's

tundra. The reality can be seen above, as a horse and droshky bring logs over the snowy and

frozen steppe to fire an engine in the winter of 1919. *Above opposite* The Eiffel Tower

dominates the 1900 *Exposition Universelle*.

and any concession to terrain ignored. Much of the development of the railroads was financed by bonds, which were quickly subscribed throughout Europe and the United States. When the Bolshevik government defaulted on the total imperial debt early in 1918, over half of it was the face value of various rail issues.

By 1884, Wagons-Lits service went from Paris to Saint Petersburg by way of the German frontier with Lithuania, where the bogies had to be changed to fit Russia's broader gauge. There were two explanations for the difference between the European and Russian gauges. The first, and most obvious, is that the ever suspicious and xenophobic Russians wanted to keep foreign rolling stock off their lines. The second was that Russian engineers had wrongly measured the European tracks, taking the outside rather than the inside width, and transferred this mistake to the tens of thousands of railway lines traversing their country. But the economical Nagelmackers decided that he might as well run his bogey-changing cars down through Europe and the Iberian Peninsula, which did not match the standard European gauge either. That is how the Nord-Sud Express from Saint Petersburg to Lisbon was born. The

Prussian kaiser quickly discovered that Nagelmackers was making a profit on his lines, and suspended his contract and the service through Wirballen for eleven years in 1885. In 1887, the enterprising Belgian changed the route, avoiding Germany by running through Vienna and Warsaw to Saint Petersburg. At Warsaw some cars split off to Moscow, so that Europeans could easily travel to Russia's two largest cities in the style to which they had become accustomed. The Russian railroads were not indifferent to their passengers' comfort. As early as 1864, they offered an early version of Pullman beds and carriages with bathrooms and even hot tubs. Moscow and Saint Petersburg both had several modern and extravagant railroad stations from which travelers headed out to the various outposts of Russia's great empire, and connections could easily be made from Moscow with Russia's main cities.

SAINT PETERSBURG

Peter the Great inaugurated his imperial capital in 1703. It was literally wrested from the marshes and

The Trans-Siberian train stops at the Ob Station at the turn of the century, and the crew lines the

platform to be photographed. The stations along the line were often far from any urban centers

and offered only slight relief from the monotony of the long voyage. The neat and small station,

with its carved wooden gingerbread, reflects the age-old characteristics of the peasant house or

izba.

built at a colossal cost in terms of human life. He wanted a port accessible all year round, and felt that a still-medieval Russia could be catapulted into modern times if her capital faced Europe and reflected Western enlightenment. He forced the Moscow nobility to build palaces on the Neva, the Moscow Patriarchate was replaced by a Ministry of Religious Affairs, Peter styled himself emperor rather than czar, and Russia's power structure quickly moved north. Peter brought the best European architects to Saint Petersburg, as did his daughter Elizabeth (1709–62), who came to the throne in 1741. To her—and Count Bartolommeo Rastrelli —we owe the Winter Palace, the summer palace at Tsarskoe Selo, and the many other pastel-colored baroque delights of the Elizabethan age. And to Catherine the Great, who ruled from 1762 to 1796, the Russians owe an age of enlightenment and the incredibly rich collections of the world-famous Hermitage.

Saint Petersburg—present-day Leningrad—shimmers with the play of light on water. It is best in mid-winter or during the mid-summer solstice when the sun never sets. Before the Revolution, the Saint Petersburg season opened at the Christmas Bazaar of the Circle of the Nobility and ended at Lent. It was an exhausting series of entertainments. Upon arrival the Belle Epoque traveler was driven through the snow and ice to one of the city's grand hotels, carried by a droshky pulled by a smart horse encouraged by the gentle pleading of a heavily bundled driver. Ice formed on his beard and sprayed from the steel runners that cut through the snow, and if the horse stood still a few minutes, his coat quickly became a solid cake of ice. The passenger, wrapped in bearskins, was kept warm by hot bricks placed on the floor of the carriage, and arrived within minutes at one of Saint Petersburg's grand hotels. The best were the Astoria, on the corner of Morskaya Street and Voznesensky Prospekt, and the Evropeiskaya (the Hotel de l'Europe), on the famous Nevsky Prospekt, which was the Fifth Avenue of Saint Petersburg. These hotels, modeled after similar great establishments in Europe, had all possible comforts and were virtual tropical gardens of exotic plants and flowers. In the overheated rooms of the best houses, hotels, and restaurants, visitors were always struck by the profusion of greenery, an escape from the long,

cold winters that gripped the city. Double windows were in all the rooms, and sand was spread between the sashes, in which were planted little horns of salt to absorb the dampness and prevent the formation of frost flowers, which would have cracked the glass. One could also stay at the more modest Hotel d'Angleterre, opposite Saint Isaac's Cathedral, and many foreigners were put up at large private houses or embassies, whose drivers and servants were clad in house livery.

Visitors immediately headed for the "Nevsky," a broad, three-mile-long boulevard that led from the Admiralty to the river to the Alexander Nevsky Monastery. Here were the finest shops and restaurants of the capital; the Nevsky was also so filled with churches of so many different denominations that it was known as "Toleration Street." A foreigner unfamiliar with Cyrillic script could immediately find his way around as the facades were often embellished with little paintings of the goods sold within (the names of the better stores were written in the Roman alphabet). Here were the splendid jewelers (the grandest of all, Fabergé, had its windows on Morskaya Street). Yeliseyev's grandiose Art Nouveau delicacy shop was bursting with round boxes of caviar, plumed game, smoked fish, imported foie gras, pastries, and Russian *pirojki*, in addition to fruits and vegetables from around the world. It had a concert hall on the second floor and buffets on the

A church at Taiga, near Tomsk, one of the main stops on the Trans-Siberian railroad.

third. Not far off was the Café Wolf et Béranger, a favorite meeting place for poets and intellectuals, and the reddish-purple Stroganov Palace, built by Rastrelli, which contained the family's important art collection and was open to the public at certain times of day. The facade of the famous Gostinni Dvor, an Oriental-type, two-floor souk where some five thousand people worked, was also on the Nevsky. It had about two hundred shops where one could buy jewels, treasures, or artifacts from Russia's far-flung empire, including precious and semiprecious stones, pearls, furs, embroideries, leather, and carvings in wood or ivory, in addition to the perfumes so copiously used by the Russian gentry. The great boulevard had French and English bookstores, fashionable hairdressers, photographers, and restaurants.

What immediately struck the traveler was the richness and variety of dress. Men were covered in medals or carried swords; students were identified by special caps; and soldiers and sailors paraded in impeccable uniforms, as did members of the imperial household. Purveyors of everything from blinis to sweets hawked their wares. Each was dressed in a traditional costume, like the bear tamers and a lady who entertained the crowds by sticking her head into the mouth of a crocodile.

At the end of the boulevard, on the river, was the imposing Admiralty building that abutted the colossal Palace Square, in the center of which Alexander I, on

top of a red Finnish granite column rising 137 feet, trampled a snake symbolizing rebellion. The Winter Palace could be entered when the imperial family was away—which was most of the time. When the family was in Saint Petersburg, ordinary citizens were allowed in limited numbers to attend the ceremonies and festivities of the court—*if* they had a frock coat. The square then came to life with the arrival and departure of ambassadors and ministers and parades of the many colorful regiments, particularly the Chevalier Guards, who were the personal bodyguards of the imperial family, chosen for their beauty and family background.

In the winter, the Neva froze solid and the droshkies crossed the ice to the outlying islands. During the coldest months, Eskimos came down from the arctic circle on reindeer sleds, set up their tepees on the ice, and made a small fortune giving rides to children and grown-ups alike. It was in this thick ice that Prince Yussupov and the Grand Duke Mikhail attempted to dispose of the body of Rasputin, whom they had just murdered.

There was no lack of things to do in the great city. There were wonderful restaurants where French chefs lent a light hand to the traditional heavy Russian cuisine. The most famous were Cubat and Medved (The Bear), and many of them had music. There were theaters, concerts, and the world-famous Imperial Ballet at the pale blue and richly gilded Marinsky Theater. Here Pavlova, Karsavina, Nijinsky, and Fokine danced the masterpieces that Marius Petipa had created in his fifty-year domination of the institution. The horses and drivers waited in the freezing night, and no sooner had the performance ended than the elegant night owls in evening dress and jewels rushed across the icy Neva to the islands for supper in restaurants where gypsies sang their deep-throated songs into the early hours of the morning. At dawn, the pleasure seekers would be carried over to the "mountains of ice," where muzhiks held gleaming torches as they sledded down the wooden ramps that had been turned into a toboggan run. From here, it was home to bed wrapped in sables and velvet.

The joys of Saint Petersburg were practically unlimited if the traveler had an introduction to a member of one of the grand and legendarily rich families—the Schuvalovs, Anichkovs, Stroganoffs, Orlovs, Lobanov-Rostovskys, or Yussupovs, whose wealth matched that

Above **The Emperor, Nicholas II, and his son, the Czarevitch Alexis, travel to the front on the**

Imperial train during World War I. The dark blue train was incredibly luxurious and in constant

danger from terrorists. *Opposite* **A view of Nevsky Prospekt, the principal shopping center of**

Saint Petersburg.

of the emperor. Tables were always set for friends, and the hospitality they extended was part of a Russian tradition that crossed over all classes of society.

MOSCOW

The train to Moscow that left from the Nicholas Station was comfortable and modern. On the way, it stopped to allow passengers the chance to assuage their hunger. Théophile Gautier gives us a very revealing glimpse of the high standards of luxury that prevailed at stations along the route, describing one at the halfway point between the two cities:

> The table was splendidly served, covered with silver and glass, and loaded down with flowers of every sort and kind. The long *quilles* of the Rhine wine towered above the bottles of Bordeaux with their slender, metal-topped corks and the bottles of champagne with their silver paper tops; all the fine brands were there

> .... the cuisine, it is scarcely necessary to say, was French.... The servants, in black with white cravats and gloves, circulated around the tables waiting attentively, though noiselessly.

> Our appetite satisfied, while the travelers were emptying their glasses of every shape, we looked at the two salons at each end of the station, reserved for illustrious personages, the elegant little shops, where were exposed sachets, shoes, slippers from Toula, of morocco embroidered with gold and silver, Circassian carpets, embroidered in silk on scarlet grounds, belts woven with gold threads, cases containing dishes of platinum inlaid with gold in exquisite taste, models of the cracked bell of the Kremlin, Russian wooden crosses...

After Saint Petersburg, Moscow was rather disappointing, particularly in the Belle Epoque. The brilliance and fun, not to speak of the government and nobility, were in the capital; Moscow was a somewhat forbidding working town. It was still the industrial and financial heart of the empire, whose life was enriched

---

A view across the Neva to the Academy of Arts in Saint Petersburg. This fine neoclassical building,

painted in a subtle shade of yellow, is one of the many official buildings lining both banks of the Neva, a busy

thoroughfare for boats in summer and horse-drawn sleds in winter. On the main banks of the Neva are

Rastrelli's splendid green and white colonnaded Winter Palace, the neoclassical Admiralty, the palaces of the

Grand Dukes and of Catherine the Great's favorite, Prince Orlov, and the smaller Dutch-style palace built by

Peter the Great, founder of one of Europe's most beautiful cities.

by a prosperous bourgeoisie. But despite its provincial character, it was home to a vibrant community of writers, actors, singers, and playwrights. It was in Moscow that Stanislavski, Meyerhold, and Vakhtangov created the modern art theater, that the merchant princes showed their Picassos and Matisses, and, in the Bolshoi Theater, that Feodor Chaliapin re-created Boris Godunov to Mussorgsky's score. There were grand hotels for rich businessmen—the National, Metropole, Dresden, and Savoy—and the leading restaurant was the multi-story Praga in the Arbat, Moscow's old quarter. Visitors then, as today, visited the Kremlin, the monasteries, and the Tretiakov Gallery. And from Moscow they could travel on comfortable trains to the unique "Golden Circle" of walled towns that had protected Moscow from

Above The CIWL offices in Moscow before 1914. ***Below*** The Riazan Station.

the barbarian invasion: Zagorsk, Yaroslavl, Rostov-Veliki, Vladimir, and Suzdal. Unlike in Saint Petersburg, the mysticism of Holy Russia still burned brightly in the ancient capital and its satellites.

ACROSS THE STEPPES

The Kazan Station in Moscow is still the starting point for the longest railroad journey in the world. The Trans-Siberian stretches 4,700 miles to Vladivostok on the Sea of Japan. The fame of the Orient Express lay in the sybaritic comfort of its accommodations, the glamour of its passengers, the variety of countries through which it passed, and the opulence of its ultimate destination on the Golden Horn. None of this was the case on the Trans-Siberian. The trains were standard, the landscape boring, and the passengers businesslike. There were quite good Russian expresses running along the line by the early years of this century, but the CIWL cars had that cosmopolitan chic that made a difference, particularly over such a long trip. At the 1900 *Exposition Universelle* in Paris, the Compagnie Internationale des Wagons-Lits issued 25,000 tickets to see the sumptuous Louis XVI-style cars destined to travel across Siberia. There was even a series of cut-away cars in which one could dine while a cyclorama of the steppes was unrolled. People marveled at the elaborate paneling, the blue-plush hangings, the hairdressing salon sheathed in sycamore, the gymnasium, and the bathrooms, not to mention the piano car designed to while away the long winter evenings singing and dancing. Very little of this matériel ever saw the steppes; CIWL decided it was not going to risk its most beautiful cars on the light and shaky lines put up as quickly and as economically as possible with mostly slave labor. Still, the company's porters and waiters always spoke several languages, the menu was more international, the compartments larger, and the atmosphere more to the liking of spoiled Westerners. They were, however, always overbooked and the Russian trains were a perfectly comfortable alternative. A traveler in 1910 described his express train:

Along the broad aisles you walk, past the staterooms, filled with baggage, littered with bedding, kettles, novels, and fur overcoats. Everything is in direst confusion, and the owners are sandwiched precariously between their belongings. On the little tables which are raised between the seats, they are playing endless games of cards, sipping tea and nonchalantly smoking cigarettes the while. You pass the stove-niches at the car entrances, heaped to the ceiling with cut wood. The fire-tenders as you pass give the military salute. You cross the covered bridges between the cars, where are little mounds of the snow that has sifted in around the crevices; and a belt of cold air tells of the zero temperature outside. At length the double doors of the foremost car appear ahead, and crossing one more arctic zone over the couplings, you can hang your fur cap by the door and salute the ikon that with ever-burning lamp looked down over the parlor-car. Now you can sit on the broad sofa set along the wall, or doze in the corner-rocker under the bookcase, or sit tete-à-tete in armchairs over a miniature table.

One of the many oddities of traveling through Siberia by train was that passengers kept their watches on Saint Petersburg time all the way to the Pacific Ocean so that they appeared to be having lunch in the evening or breakfast late at night. On the Trans-Siberian, passengers could mostly look forward to weeks of dreary and monotonous tundra punctuated by occasional scrub and a forest of birch trees. The trip was particularly monotonous in the winter, when a great white blanket covered the few distinguishing features of the landscape—an onion-cupola church, a few painted wooden *izbas*, a stone fortress. Passengers killed time chatting, drinking tea, playing cards, eating for hours, and drinking endless glasses of vodka and Russian brandy. The train, for reasons never really explained, did not even stop in the few cities en route, as the railroad stations had been placed several miles away from them. The most plausible explanation is that the *kuptsi*, or merchants, refused to cough up the ransom the bureaucracy demanded for enriching their urban centers with the pocketbooks of the travelers on the expresses crossing the country. Those who did visit Siberian towns on the way were generally disappointed. They were nothing more than outposts, generally designed along horizontal and vertical axes, and the

Top and right Cars of the Trans-Siberian Railroad

exhibited at the Paris Expo of 1900. Designed in

the Russian taste, they never saw service along the

line. For comparison, note the slightly more sober

types of stock and buildings (*center and left*) which

were generally in use in Russia at the time.

provincial local society dreamed only of leaving for Moscow or Saint Petersburg.

BUILDING THE GREAT RAILROAD

The most admirable attribute of the Trans-Siberian line was that it existed, not that a few privileged people could travel along it in luxury. One of the earliest pioneers who attempted to build this great lifeline through the Russian wilderness was an American, Perry McDonough Collins, who arrived in Saint Petersburg on May 19, 1856. He crossed Siberia by sled, proposed a $20,000,000 stock scheme to "construct a railroad from Chita to Irkutsk by the Amur Railroad Company," and never got his project off the ground. For thirty years the project lay idle until a line was extended from Perm to Ekaterinburg across the Urals, the mountainous frontier dividing Asiatic Siberia from European Russia. In 1885 and 1886, Count Alexis P. Ignatyev, then governor of the large Irkutsk province, informed the powers in distant Saint Petersburg that large numbers of Chinese were invading the Transbaikal, and that if the imperial troops could not be sent out in short order to stem the tide, Siberia's riches might soon cease to swell the coffers of the Russian imperial city. He also pointed out that such a line would seriously aid in Siberia's development. Alexander III, the large and visionary emperor, saw the point and got the project going. The line was to run along the 55th parallel, since all of Siberia's arable land (about 10 percent of the entire land mass) lies between the parallels of 55° and 58°30' north latitude. The cost of the enterprise was to be so great that many feared it would bankrupt Russia. In late May 1891 Alexander's son Nicholas—the last Russian emperor—dug his silver spade into a wheelbarrow, and dumped the first earth on an embankment that was to be the beginning of the Ussuri line to Khabarovsk.

There was a master plan for the Trans-Siberian, the world's longest and most audacious railway. It was to be built in several sections, with specified deadlines. The West Siberian Line went from Chelyabinsk to Novosibirsk via Omsk, the Mid-Siberian Line through Tomsk and Krasnoyarsk to Irkutsk in the vicinity of Lake Baikal. The commission then envisaged the Trans-Baikal via Chita to Sretensk, and from there along the Amur River to Khabarovsk and down the Ussuri line to Vladivostok.

The first section passed mostly through the Kirgiz steppe, a dreary and flat wasteland that could not even supply the timber for the ties or the stones for the embankment, all of which had to be brought in. The second section, the Mid-Siberian, passed through more difficult and mountainous terrain, ending up on the southeastern tip of Lake Baikal, the world's largest and deepest reservoir of fresh water.

LAKE BAIKAL

Baikal is 395 miles long, fifty miles broad at its widest, and over a mile deep in parts. Until recently, it was the least polluted lake in the world, although fed by over three hundred rivers and mountain streams. Lake Baikal is the scenic highlight of the Trans-Siberian trip and has always excited the passengers who have crossed it or traveled along its shores. In the summer, its waters are so clear that one can see clearly down through more than a hundred feet, and it contains prehistoric species of fish that are extinct elsewhere. Lake Baikal is also the only body of fresh water to contain large schools of seal that have most probably swum down from the arctic circle over the millennia, gradually

A watercolor by N. Karazine, c.1890, showing convicts making their way through the snows of Siberia. The convict system in Russia was particularly cruel, and hundreds of thousands of people were deported beyond the Urals on the slightest pretext. Many died, some escaped, and a few were freed and settled in the great wilderness. Convicts were much used as slave labor on the Trans-Siberian Railway, and the line was used to transport carloads of prisoners to exile.

Opposite The church car of the Trans-Siberian, built at the express wish of the Emperor Nicholas II who felt it inappropriate for his subjects to travel long distances without religious succor.

adapting from salt to fresh water. Great granite cliffs rise from its blue waters, their peaks forever covered in snow, and beautiful alpine flowers grow on its shores. The air and sky are incredibly clear in the short summer season, after which the lake quickly ices over. The commission planned to continue the line along the southeastern shore of the lake. The lake's southern end, however, required endless tunnels and bridges for railroad passage, and as a first step the commission decided to cross the lake by means of a large icebreaking ferry.

On December 30, 1895, a contract was signed with Sir W. G. Armstrong's Walker Shipyard at Newcastle-upon-Tyne for the *Baikal*, a 4,200-ton, 295-foot monster icebreaker. Its hull was belted with inch-thick steel plates and reinforced by a two-foot inner sheathing of timber. The *Baikal* could accommodate an entire express train and had a bronze forescrew under her prow to stir up the water under the four-foot-thick ice, which would then be cracked with incredible noise by the heavy hull. The *Baikal* could also carry twenty-eight fully loaded freight cars on three pairs of rails, and had cabins for 150 passengers plus lounges, restaurants, and a fully equipped Orthodox church. The whole ship was sent in pieces along Siberia's rivers, as was a smaller icebreaking ferry, the *Nagara*, in 1898, which is still in service today. It all worked beautifully in summer and early winter. However, when the ice started to get thicker, the large *Baikal* was used simply to crash ahead and open up a channel for the *Nagara*, and on many occasions everything stopped in the middle of the lake, where the passengers disembarked and were carried to the shore and a new train by sled.

COMPLETING THE LINE

The great impetus to the building of the line was given by Count Sergei Witte, when he was appointed head of the Trans-Siberian commission in early 1892. He was also appointed communications minister and finance minister in the same year, and became prime minister of the country, which was modernized, largely thanks to his genius, in 1905. Witte immediately saw the Trans-Siberian project as a way to open up a large land mass to a hemmed-in peasantry, as a means of transporting labor to Siberia's incredibly rich mines, and of bringing their production to the Pacific and Atlantic alike. It was also a perfectly viable alternative to the new transport routes opened up by the Suez Canal, and a way of checking Japanese and Chinese ambitions by being able to transport troops to the far end of the empire in weeks rather than months. Witte hoodwinked the Chinese into agreeing to let him build the Trans-Manchurian line through their territory, which not only cut over 1,000 miles off the planned line but also brought the Russian Bear through Mukden to Port Arthur and Dalny (Dairen), where it had access to a year-round port by means of a spur off the main line.

In 1905 the Trans-Baikal loop was completed, and the 1,200-mile Amur line was built between 1908 and 1916, opening up another vast piece of wilderness.

Convicts were put to work on the line, as there was no ready source of labor willing to undertake the backbreaking job of building railroad tracks on terrain that shifted constantly from ice to slush to desert. They would face death from anthrax, cholera, smallpox, or plague, and risk maulings by Siberian tigers or packs of wild wolves. Not only were they paid, but their sentences were substantially shortened on a formula fixed by the government.

The line was already a success at the beginning of the century. The number of carloadings on the Chelyabinsk–Irkutsk section was more than four times the original estimate, and Russians emigrated at a steady pace. The government allotted about 140 acres of arable land, exemption from military service and taxes, interest-free loans for farm equipment and seed, and cheap transport to the new frontier to each family that moved there. Conditions were not ideal, but there was a hospital car on the end of each immigrant train, and by 1898 the mortality of settlers in transit had been reduced from 20 per cent before the advent of the line to .005 per cent afterward. There were not only people to till the soil, but miners, engineers, and skilled laborers to exploit the natural riches and build a new industrial base. The worker gradually replaced the prisoners but Siberia will always evoke an image of suffering and injustice.

Сибирь.—Sibérie. № 102.
Наружный видъ вагона-церкви.—La vue extérieure du wagon-église.

229 Pyramide Cheops: Ascension

EGYPT

The pyramid at Cheops at Giza around
1880. Once faced with marble that was
removed to build Cairo's mosques, the
underlying structure of the pyramid
allowed tourists to climb to the
top—usually with the help of guides.

A trip to Egypt was the most exciting of all the winter activities available to the rich at the turn of the century. The Egyptian "season" was from Christmas to early spring, and liners crossed to Alexandria filled with adventurers in search of an answer to the riddle of the Sphinx. They found in Cairo the world of a thousand and one nights, bazaars filled with precious carpets, jewelry, and sweet spices, streets abounding with processions of dervishes, veiled ladies, and gentlemen in bright red fezzes. In the nearby desert they were dazzled by the pyramids of Giza and Memphis, and once they started on a trip up the Nile, they found themselves in the land of the Bible and the pharaohs. This odd mixture of fantasy, treasure hunt, and the occult in Egypt has had an extraordinary appeal to travelers from all periods and places, from the days of ancient Rome to the present.

A traveler at the end of the nineteenth century found a very different Egypt than can be discovered today. Alexandria was then a thriving city of remarkable luxury with a highly cosmopolitan population of Greeks, Jews, Cypriots, Italians, and Arabs. It was a vibrant center of trade, and French was its second language

—as it was in Cairo. People had grown rich trading cotton, shipping goods around the world, doing deals, and being wily. Alexandria was Beirut before its time, and at sumptuous dinner parties served by Nubians in striped silk djellabas, the latest gossip of Paris, London, Baghdad, and Cairo was exchanged in all languages simultaneously, the babble of tongues transformed by the lilting singsong of Arabic inflection. Eastern warmth and hospitality melded with the reserved sophistication of Europe, and romance was ever present in the warm Mediterranean nights. For the tourist, Alexandria offered little. The great lighthouse at Pharos, whose guiding beam was so strong that it was purported to be able to burn a ship a hundred miles away, had disappeared. Also gone were the famous library and university to which scholars from the entire world had flocked before the birth of Christ. Anthony and Cleopatra had lived here and were buried somewhere nearby in a lost tomb, and it was to Alexandria that Menelaus brought Helen after the fall of Troy. With the sights gone, visitors bathed at San Stefano and Stanley Bay, window-shopped on elegant boulevards, went to the casino dressed in white tie and tails, and waited for the next dinner party or the luxury train to Cairo.

Egypt's capital was only a few hours away in the elegant CIWL car, and travelers expecting the excitement of the desert were sorely disappointed. Egypt has often been compared to a fan with a thin handle. The handle is, of course, the Nile that flows through the parched desert, bringing life and prosperity with it. Through the great deserts of brown and black rocks and yellow sand, the Nile cuts a thin ribbon of green. After it reaches Cairo, it fans out into the delta, carrying with it the rich silt of the African land mass. The result is one of the richest farming areas in the world, a large territory of patches of cotton and vegetables, of waving fields of grain tilled by peasants in ageless methods dating back to biblical times. In this small area between Egypt's two largest cities was half the country's arable land.

THE LEGENDARY SHEPHEARD'S
Upon arrival at Cairo Station, an elegant stone terminus up to the highest European standards, the

Above **Posters of CIWL advertising tours to Egypt and the Near East. The opening of the Suez Canal in 1869 marked the true beginning of tourism in Egypt, which rapidly developed into the status trip for the winter season. The warm climate, exotic cities, historic ruins and appeal of a slow boat trip made up an irresistible package. CIWL and Cook's were bitter rivals for the ever-increasing tourist trade, and both quickly built or brought hotels, steamers and railroad concessions.** *Opposite* **The Temple of Amun at Karnak photographed by Bonfils, *c.*1880.**

Bonfils

Souvenir du Shepheard's Hotel Cairo·

casino and then taken over by CIWL in 1894. It became one of the finest hotels in Cairo after Shepheard's, which CIWL also took over shortly afterward. Shepheard's guests followed Kipling's adage that "East is East and West is West, and never the twain shall meet." They were willing to temporarily leave its cool, European interior to venture out first by donkey and later by taxi into the tumultuous city, but they fully expected every Western comfort upon their return; that included French cuisine, Swiss chambermaids, and the offices of Thomas Cook and Son to smooth out all the discomforts and problems posed by life and movement in the land of the infidel.

passenger looked out for the uniformed representative of the legendary Shepheard's, a hotel that justifiably had earned its reputation as the center of European life in the Middle Eastern capital. Converted from a harem, it had opened in 1841 and served as Napoleon's headquarters during the Egyptian campaign. Located outside the old city walls on Ezbekiyah Boulevard, now known as El-Gumhuriya Street, it was considerably enlarged in 1891, and was further extended by popular demand in 1899, 1904, 1909, and 1927. As of 1891, it had its famous veranda on the boulevard, filled with rattan chairs and tables, sheltered by a striped awning under which tourists watched the teeming life of the Middle Eastern city with unending fascination.

Nearby were the beautiful Ezbekiyah Gardens and the new Opera House, which had been built in 1869 to coincide with the festivities associated with the opening of the Suez Canal. Many of Europe's monarchs arrived on their yachts to help the khedive celebrate this important moment in Egypt's history, but the most glamorous guest was the Empress Eugénie, for whom the Gezirah Palace was built in 1869 by Ismail Pasha so that she and other monarchs could live in the style to which they were accustomed. The khedive practically bankrupted the state with his bash, for which Giuseppe Verdi was commissioned to write *Aida* (he did not finish in time, and the small, lovely Opera House opened with *Rigoletto* instead). As a consequence, the Gezirah Palace was first made into a

THOMAS COOK

Egypt was Thomas Cook's apotheosis, the high point of a career that launched travel as an industry. This messianic, church-loving, and prohibitionist Englishman was as important to the history of travel as Henry Ford was to the development of the automobile. To bring boatloads of people to the land of the Bible (his

Shepheard's was synonymous with Cairo to most luxury travelers and grew to accommodate the increasing

tourist trade. Its facade (*above*), was on a busy thoroughfare, Ezbekiyah Boulevard, but its

large garden (*opposite*), was an oasis of peace in the dusty confusion of the Egyptian capital.

There were other luxury hotels, particularly the Gezirah Palace built to house the Empress Eugénie

and other monarchs at the time of the inauguration of the Suez Canal. But Shepheard's was the

symbol of the foreigner's outpost and was appropriately put to the flame in a nationalistic uprising in 1952.

Egyptian excursions nearly always included Palestine and Syria) was the validation of a lifetime of hard work. Cook had his first vision at the age of thirty-three on a train between Harborough and Leicester. "What a glorious thing it would be," he later wrote, "if the newly developed powers of the railways and locomotives could be made subservient to the cause of Temperance." It was far better to distract people on a train than to allow them to while away their leisure time drinking cheap gin out of sheer boredom and desperation with urban life. He gathered up 570 passengers and took them on a day's outing by Midland Rail on July 5, 1841, from Leicester to Loughborough, where various temperance groups had set up colorful tents with refreshments (obviously nonalcoholic) and a band. The whole event made a great deal of noise, the railroad companies pursued Mr. Cook with blocks of unsold seats, and he filled them with the new urbanites who wanted to see Britain. In short order, Thomas Cook was shipping excursionists in large quantities to the spas and seaside resorts of Great Britain on their holidays, an activity much criticized by their employers, who felt that they should be resting and praying at home in preparation for Monday morning. "Surely there can be nothing inimical to religion in going abroad to behold the handiwork of the Great Supreme," retorted the busy Mr. Cook. His greatest achievement came in 1851, when he brought 165,000 people by train from all over Britain to see the Great Exhibition of that year in the Crystal Palace. For most he not only provided transport but organized lodging and meals, taking care of his charges totally from the moment they left home until they returned.

The Cook's tour—and, alas, mass-tourism—had been born, much to the dismay of the elite, who now had to put up with the hordes. There was soon a magazine, *The Excursionist*, to describe the tours and suggest other distractions, and in 1855 Mr. Cook was off with the hoi polloi to the Paris exhibition of that year. There was a predominance of single ladies on that trip, one of whom, a Miss Matilda, wrote in her diary that "Many of our friends thought us too independent and adventurous to leave the shores of England, and thus plunge into foreign lands not beneath Victoria's sway, with no protecting relative ... but we would venture

anywhere with such a guide and guardian as Mr. Cook, for there was not one of his party but felt perfectly safe under his care." Within short order, Cook's charges were taken all over Europe, crossed the Alps to Italy, and did the grand tour that had formerly been the preserve of Britain's aristocracy. Cook had moved his clientele up from the working class to the new middle class who wanted to see the world with the great

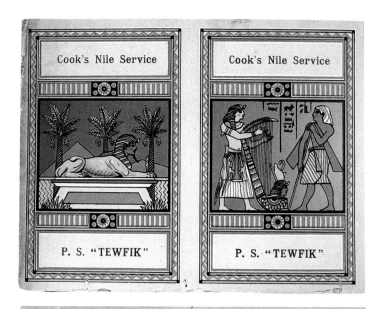

Left Thomas Cook (1808–1892), the founder of modern travel, was the pioneer of tours to the Near East and played a dominant role in the development of the Egyptian travel industry. Cook once owned all the steamers plying the Nile and was proprietor of Shepheard's where he kept an active office to serve his large clientele. His steamers had all the comforts of the contemporary transatlantic liner, and provided their guests with lists of their fellow passengers (*above*).

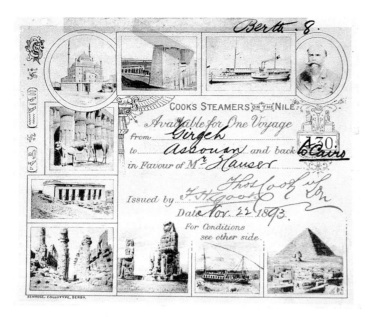

curiosity that exemplified the times. Cook's son, John Mason, was as busy as his father, and an office in Ludgate was quickly opened to serve the needs of the successful enterprise. Shortly thereafter, a network of offices sprouted up throughout Europe, hotels were built and eventually bought to serve the new clients, and the Cook representative with smart cap and livery was soon a fixture on every rail platform of Europe.

Once Cook was in Italy, there was no stopping his progress south. In 1869, the Prince and Princess of Wales—like everybody else—sailed for Egypt. The now great Thomas Cook received an invitation from his friend, Ferdinand de Lesseps, to be present at the opening of the Suez Canal, and the excursionist took along sixty tourists to share in the fun and literally follow in the wake of their beloved prince, as he and his wife made their way up the Nile. The trip started in Palestine and Syria, where the group was quickly dubbed "Hum Kukiyejeh" by the Arabs. "Kuki" organized twenty-one sleeping tents, three dining tents, and field kitchens to turn out and serve the roast mutton and breakfast eggs to which his charges were accustomed. There were sixty-seven saddle horses, eighty-seven packhorses, hordes of mules, and fifty-six muleteers to chase in the tracks of Moses and his burning bush. For safety, there were several guards and barking

dogs, and for guidance a few dragomen, the guides who always accompanied foreigners throughout the Near East, resolving myriad day-to-day problems, as well as remarking on the sights. The tourists got through the desert adventure with no problems whatsoever, and arrived at Shepheard's just before the opening of the canal and the arrival of the Prince of Wales. As usual, the Cook's tour was right on schedule.

CAIRO

At Shepheard's there was a rather obvious schism between the Cookites and the more elegant and sophisticated clients who looked down with unhidden scorn at the less privileged trippers. Notwithstanding this, the attractions of Cairo were much the same for both, except that the grander tourists had entrée to the elegant houses and receptions of Cairo's beys and pashas — perhaps even to the court of the khedive. The khedive was, in effect, a viceroy of the Ottoman sultan and ran an elaborate court along the lines of an Oriental potentate. Living in the Abdine Palace in a state of great opulence, he and his courtiers were dressed in the traditional "Stambul," a black frock coat and a fez. It was Ismail Pasha, under whose aegis the Suez Canal was created, who decreed that Egypt was part of Europe and instituted reforms that modernized the country and changed the very core of its social structure.

It was the foreign consuls of Egypt, or the khedive, who brought important foreigners into the cloying life of Egypt's upper classes. Prior to the opening of the Suez Canal, ladies of the most sophisticated houses still lived in the harem together with their husband's other wives, widowed aunts, hairy chinned grandmothers, and any other stray ladies fortunate enough to have a direct connection. Upon arrival at an elaborate palace in old Cairo, the foreign wife would be taken to the harem for tea and sweets, surrounded by plump and pale-skinned ladies who always kept away from the direct light in the farthermost recesses of their rooms. The husband, meanwhile, would go to the main houses, where conversation generally turned

A Cook's ticket for a

round-trip excursion from

Cairo to Aswan, dated

November 22, 1893,

illustrating the highlights

of an Egyptian tour.

around gambling and Arab stallions, the two favorite distractions of Egypt's beys and pashas, who were ready to stake their entire fortunes at the track or on the green felt of the roulette table. The host would later entertain his guests by taking them in his calèche, mounted by liveried servants, to the Promenade de Choubrah where "*le tout Caire*" took the air in late afternoon, and then for tea to Groppi's or other *pâtissiers* in the town.

By the turn of the century, when ladies were more liberated, they were dressed by Paris couturiers and covered in dazzling jewels, and finally joined their husbands in receiving foreigners of note in grand, new European-style palaces on the shores of the Nile. There elaborate dinners and entertainments were organized with belly dancers, singers, and Oriental delights served by liveried bearers on solid-gold plate; the festivities went on until dawn, when breakfast was served and the guests finally retired to the great hotels and palaces of Cairo. Another distraction for the grand traveler was the Gezirah Sporting Club, on an island in the middle of the Nile. This essentially British institution was off limits to Egyptians, even of the royal family, unless they were particularly skilled athletes, but foreigners whiled away the afternoon at tennis, cricket, or polo, or sunning themselves by the pool.

The premier attraction of Cairo was its extraordinarily colorful life. A contemporary traveler, Amelia B.

A poster for the Heliopolis Palace Hotel by Dorival, printed in 1910. Heliopolis is a suburb of Cairo

on the site of the oldest settlement of the city once known as Or, which was the center of the worship

of the sun God Re. The Persians razed the city to the ground in 525 BC, and moved the capital

of Egypt to Alexandria, in fact changing the desert kingdom to a Mediterranean, rather than

an African, country. By the turn of the last century, Heliopolis was a fashionable residential area,

and the Heliopolis Palace Hotel removed tourists from the dust and rush of Old Cairo.

Edwards, captured the excitement of the capital in 1877, as she waited for a procession of pilgrims on the way to Mecca:

> The place was like a fair with provision-stalls, swings, story-tellers, serpent-charmers, cake-sellers, sweetmeat-sellers, sellers of sherbet, water, lemonade, sugared nuts, fresh dates, hard-boiled eggs, oranges, and sliced water-melon. Veiled women carrying little bronze Cupids of children astride upon the right shoulder, swarthy Egyptians, coal-black Abyssinians, Arabs and Nubians of every shade from golden-brown to chocolate, fellahs, dervishes, donkey-boys, street urchins, and beggars with every imaginable deformity, came and went; squeezed themselves in and out among the carriages; lined the road on each side of the great towered gateway; swarmed on the top of every wall; and filled the air with laughter, a Babel of dialects, and those odours of Araby that are inseparable from an Eastern crowd.

Among the pilgrims were the dervishes, who not only whirled but flagellated their bodies, chanted themselves into a stupor, and were lined up rib to rib in a long and straight carpet over which a sheikh galloped on a particularly heavy horse. Those who did not survive—reputedly because of lack of sufficient faith in Allah—were carted off to the thirteen-mile-

long City of the Dead, a seemingly unending landscape of fez-shaped earthen tombs that—from the top of a distant minaret—looked like a rather bad case of the hives. The bazaars were teeming with life and exotic goods, with carpets, spices, jewelry, and (mostly fake) antiquities produced on an industrial scale in Luxor. The favorite buys were "Old Kingdom" turquoise-colored scarabs and "sheptis" given a splendid patina by a quick passage through the intestinal tracts of ducks or turkeys, and small fragments of carvings purportedly scooped from the walls of pharaonic tombs.

Great and original pieces, as well as whole mummies, stolen from the tombs were, in fact, available at reputable Cairo dealers who had given the necessary baksheesh at the top level of the office of the Service des Antiquités, and serious European and American collectors replenished their collections on annual pilgrimages. Foreign museums and institutions of learning were in charge of specific excavations and were allowed to carry off a specified portion of their loot, the lion's share going to the newly built Egyptian Museum, which was another of the great attractions of Cairo and an essential learning experience prior to going up the Nile. It was here that the tourist had his first confusing encounter with the long dynastic line of the kings and queens of ancient Egypt, the panoply of gods and goddesses, and the once-impenetrable world of hieroglyphics and the pictograph. As of the end of the

Above Anna Pavlova on the Shepheard's Terrace in 1923. The legendary ballerina was only one

of many celebrities attracted by the wonders of Ancient Egypt. *Below* A street in old Cairo

around 1900. The teeming life of the old city fascinated tourists who combed its bazaars for

bargains and watched processions of pilgrims and dervishes making their way through the

narrow and pungent streets. Cairo was rich in Islamic art and architecture, and to a nineteenth-

century visitor must have seemed straight out of *A Thousand and One Nights*.

century, he could also see the embarrassingly exposed mummies of many of Egypt's legendary pharaohs—Seti I, Thutmose II and III, Sounounri and Ahmose I (the conquerors of Syria and Ethiopia), Seti I, and Ramses II, who had been immortalized by Greek historians as Sesostris. They had been hidden, along with many royal relatives, over three thousand years earlier and were discovered by grave robbers in 1871–72 in the middle of a mountain at Deir-el-Bahri near the Valley of the Kings at Thebes. It was thanks to the French archaeologist Gaston Maspero that they were moved to Luxor in 1881, and from there to Cairo's Egyptian Museum. The other glory at the museum was the treasure of Tutankhamen, who had ruled Egypt for a few years beginning in 1357 B.C. This minor pharaoh's tomb and treasure were discovered by Howard Carter in 1922 and unearthed that year in the presence of his patron, the Earl of Carnarvon. This seemingly endless flow of jewels, furniture, artifacts, carved figures, and multilayered gold sarcophagi is the most complete

The highlights of a trip to Egypt were a visit to the pyramids and Sphinx at Giza (*above*) and a trip up the Nile

(*opposite*). By 1905, the Sphinx had mostly been excavated; thirty years earlier only its head stuck out of the

sand. A medium-size and well-heeled group, such as these German tourists (*above*), would probably have

rented their own ship, such as the fairly large dahabiyeh (*opposite*), with a large crew, which permitted a

degree of independence impossible on Cook's faster and meticulously programmed steamers. People of

leisure could take several months to explore the Nile Valley in the comfort of their own sailboats.

collection ever discovered of the panoply surrounding an ancient monarch.

Cairo was also rich in such Islamic treasures of architecture as the Mosque of Sultan Hassan, the ancient University of Al Azhan, and the tombs of the caliphs. It also boasted handsome Coptic churches, and nearby were Heliopolis, the ancient City of the Sun, and the pyramids of Giza and their Sphinx. It was to the latter, an hour and a half from Shepheard's by horse and carriage, that every tourist went, drawn by the mystery of these gigantic structures put up from great blocks of stone before even the advent of the wheel or hoist. Originally covered in marble (which had been carted off to build the five hundred mosques and many palaces of Cairo), the pyramids provided a seemingly endless progression of steps up which the traveler—protected from the heat by a pith helmet —was pulled by eager Arab guides looking for a baksheesh. Then, as now, tourists crawled into the narrow, dank, and hot corridors leading to the tombs in the innermost recesses of the pyramid, which had been stripped thousands of years before by grave robbers. It was under the unchanging glance of the Nubian-faced Sphinx— probably Cheops (or Khufu), the builder of the Great Pyramid—that tourists had their first encounter with a camel. Belching, groaning, gnashing its teeth, the apparently formless brown lump waited for tourists to sit in his wooden saddle before springing up with a violent shake that invariably caused hysterics or hilarity. A photographer always had a supply of glass plates to record the occasion, and attics today shelter the obligatory photograph of great-grandparents teetering on their dromedary.

Near the pyramids was the famous Mena House, one of Egypt's most luxurious institutions, where one had tea or drinks on the lovely terrace while watching the pyramids change into infinite shades of yellow, gold, brown, and gray as the sun set, casting a mile-long shadow of the pyramids over the ever-shifting sands of the desert. The Mena House was named after a pharaoh who had united Upper and Lower Egypt in a single empire, and was an enchanting base from which not only to slowly absorb the awesome mysteries of Giza—the Great Pyramid of Cheops, the Second Pyramid of Chephren (Khafre), the Third Pyramid of

Mycerinus (Menkaure), and the Sphinx—but also to visit the nearby pyramids of Dahshur and Saqqarah. Arab horses would be saddled up for Mena House guests at any time of day or night for a gallop into the desert, and upon their return there was the bliss of a hot bath, a drink among more antique Oriental furnishings, and dinner in the moonlight to the sound of gypsy violins. Within riding distance was Fayum and the ancient Egyptian capital of Memphis, and many travelers spent weeks at Mena House visiting the desert and absorbing the curative rays of Egypt's endless winter sun.

A TRIP UP THE NILE

The penultimate joy of a trip to Egypt, however, was a trip up the Nile. It was along the banks of the life-giving river that the traveler was suddenly immersed in the immutable life of Egypt, that he or she became absorbed by the strange and morbid search for an afterlife or simply enjoyed lazy days cruising through an ever-changing landscape while basking in the sun. The dryness of the desert climate and its fine sand miraculously preserved the secrets of a dead civilization throughout the millennia. At the turn of the century it was by no means unusual for a traveler to come upon, or even fall into, a tomb that had lain undiscovered since it was created. The carvings would be as sharp and the wall paintings as brilliant as they were on the

A Wagon-Lits carriage is loaded on a boat to Egypt in 1928.

CIWL was very active in developing comfortable travel along

the Nile; a service went from Alexandria or Port Said to Cairo,

another from Cairo to Aswan, and a third from Cairo to

Khartoum, through the Sudan. The Sudan train was painted

white, and the service lasted through World War II.

day the chamber received its dead mummy in search of eternal life. There was a great sense of discovery, and Egypt was still being dug out. Photographs of the Sphinx in 1860 reveal only a puzzled head sticking out of the sand; thirty years later, only one claw was pawing on the ground. At the end of the century, Abu Simbel was largely buried in sand, and a great desert cascade separated Ramses II from the small temple to his queen, Nefertiri; the funerary temple of Queen Hatshepsut was being excavated by the Metropolitan Museum; the temple of Kom Ombo was buried practically up to the capitals of its columns. There was still a certain casual attitude to the process of excavation, and travelers could freely pocket bits of ancient pottery or glass from the rubble, and observe exciting changes from year to year.

Nobody was yet in a hurry; a steamer trip took at least three weeks from Cairo to Aswan, a voyage by sail anywhere from six to twelve, depending on the winds and the disposition of the passengers. The slowness of peasant life, the gentle flow of the river, the pleasant days and cool nights, the brilliance of the sun, and crystalline shape of the moon made time pass with incredible speed as the ships plied up and down the life-giving river. In historical terms, one sailed up the Nile starting with the early monuments in Cairo and ending up in Abu Simbel after negotiating the rocky first cataract at Aswan; the archaeological highlight of the trip was Luxor, where a grand hotel refreshed passengers fed up with the constrictions of boat life. As the Nile flowed north, one sailed "up" it heading south, always the cause of substantial confusion to tourists.

British tourists posing in front of the Temple of Karnak in Luxor toward the turn of the century.

On the far right, in buttoned livery, is Cook's representative, and seated on ancient stones on

the far left are the group's dragomen, local guides who explained the ruins. The women's heavy

dresses would seem to belie the gentlemen's pith helmets. Feigning hardship in the desert,

however, was part of the romance of travel. The English formed the largest contingent of

travelers to Egypt in the Belle Epoque and financed important excavations.

The boats unloaded one group of passengers from Cairo at Aswan and picked up another heading north, and travel agents made sure that their boats were filled throughout the season, which lasted from November to early April. Passengers could be quickly transported to and from Cairo by an inland train, and, as of 1898, CIWL provided sleepers with double roofs and slats over the windows: the dining cars were cooled to 77°F when the outside temperature hovered around 100°F thanks to air blown over three hundred pounds of ice. Originally known as the Cairo–Luxor Express, the all-Pullman train was renamed the Star of Egypt when the service was extended to Aswan a few years later. There were many passengers who simply took the train to Luxor or Aswan where they spent the winter, much as people today winter in Palm Springs or Marrakesh.

The dedicated tourist, however, had to go at least one way by ship and there were essentially three types of boats that cruised the Nile: the cangia, the dahabiah, and later the steamboat. The cangia was immortalized by Gustave Flaubert, who hired one to sail up the Nile with his friend, the photographer Maxime du Camp, in 1849. While du Camp busily prepared his glass plates, which provide us with some of the earliest —and most splendid—pictures of early Egypt, Flaubert eagerly pursued ladies (and boys) of all colors, leaving behind a detailed account of hot nights in the company of belly dancers and prostitutes, proudly describing the intensity and frequency of his copulations. Flaubert's cangia was painted blue, had a crew of nine, a saloon with two little divans facing each other, another room with two beds, and a small room for their servant, a Corsican ex-dragoon named Sassetti. Their dragoman, Giuseppe Brichetti, slept on deck along with the crew, headed by Rais Ibrahim, a young man of twenty-four. Larger than the cangia was the dahabiah, but both were propelled exclusively by sail, were flat-bottomed, and had living quarters built at the

Above **The Hotel Cataract at Aswan in 1915. This riverside palace remains quite unchanged today: its dark public rooms are still filled with nineteenth-century books on ancient Egypt, its colorfully tented terrance still shelters tea-drinking tourists watching the flow of the dark waters of the Nile around the smooth rocks. Aswan, unlike Luxor, was a full-fledged resort where people spent the entire winter. *Opposite* A group of tourists, *c.*1900, picnic at the entrance of a tomb watched over by their servant and dragoman. There was a great sense of exploration, and travelers were often present at the discovery of hidden tombs and ruins.**

stern on top of the deck. When the wind died down or the water level was low and the river became an obstacle course of sandbars, the crew would leap into the river and pull the ship along by rope, suffering cuts, bruises, and occasionally broken bones as a result. The crew lived simply, eating only hardtack softened by river water into a mush, and they baked their biscuits periodically on special wood stoves set out on the riverbank.

Amelia Edwards, who went up the Nile with friends, describes the delights of her large dahabiah: it had a skylighted dining room with walls of white wainscoting highlighted in gold, a saloon with a piano and cushioned divans lining the walls, several comfortable bedrooms, and a crew consisting of a captain, steersman, dragoman, twelve sailors, two cooks, and two sailors, all of whom were in a perpetually good mood despite the hardship of their lives. At dawn and at dusk, the men went off to shoot pigeons for dinner, and by day the boats sailed on the river, stopping at

the many temples on or near the shore. In the evening the ships anchored, the cook turned out a remarkable variety of European and Oriental dishes, and the sailors sang their whining songs as the sky slowly became a velvet blanket sewn with glistening stars.

Less romantic, but far more comfortable, were the paddle steamers belonging to Thomas Cook. They had all the comforts of a grand hotel: large public rooms, nondescript international cuisine, English newspapers and magazines, a promenade deck covered by an awning, white-robed and white-gloved servants wearing red fezzes and cummerbunds, and a doctor in case of malaise in a foreign land. In the evening the men dressed in white tie and tails, the ladies in long evening dresses, their shoulders covered in fur wraps against the cold night air of the desert. These British-built steamers isolated the traveler from the brutality as well as the delights of the world outside, and were only stopped by the *hamsin*, a violent windstorm that turned the Nile into a stormy channel whose waves were covered with a sandy foam. Great columns of sand then rose into the sky, the sun was blotted out, and everyone nearly suffocated in the gritty heat.

Regardless of the means of transport, the itinerary was fixed, as it all lay along the banks of the river. The first stop was at the rock tombs of Beni Hassan, the only large mortuary complex on the east bank of the Nile. Then came Tell el 'Amarna, the land of Akhenaten and his queen, Nefertiti, who were well known through the king's hermaphroditic and realistic portraits in the Cairo Museum and the queen's magnificent bust in Berlin. Farther down was Assiut, the capital of Egypt in the nineteenth century, and Abydos, the traditional burial site of the god Osiris. By this time, the passengers felt quite friendly and familiar with the confusing hierarchy of ancient Egypt's gods and kings and were ready for the astonishing treasures in and around Luxor. It was on the banks of this ancient city that the boats reunited, flying the flags of their charterers, who visited each other for tea, cocktails, and dinner after visiting Luxor's Temple of Amenhotep, the Great Temple of Amun at Karnak—the largest religious building ever constructed—the Temple of Hathor at Dendarah with its portrait of Cleopatra, and the astonishing tombs in the Valley of the

A dragoman deciphers hieroglyphics. It was thanks to the Rosetta stone, discovered in 1799,

and presently in the British Museum, that the code to the puzzling pictographs of Egypt's

ancient civilization was finally cracked by the brilliant French archaeologist Jean-François

Champollion. Thereafter, the profusely carved exteriors of Egypt's temples and tombs told the

world of the history and achievements of the pharaohs. One might doubt the deciphering

abilities of the dragomen above, but tourists are always ready to believe what they are told.

Kings, the great mortuary complex on the other side of the river. Also here were Medinat Habu and the mortuary temple of Ramses III; the fallen statue of Ozymandias, Shelley's "King of Kings"; and the Colossi of Amenhotep III sitting totally alone in the desert, each of their fingers the length of a grown man. They were supposed to emit a singing sound at night, but few tourists could brave the other bad vibrations emanating from this lugubrious death center. It was far jollier to return to the terrace of the Luxor Palace for drinks, dinner on monogrammed gold plate, and dancing on the terrace.

The wonders in and around Luxor took at least a week to see in those slower times, and the passengers would then head off toward Aswan, first stopping at Esna, where there was a splendid bazaar and a brisk trade in slaves and donkeys. From here, the landscape started to change: the riverbank was steeper, the mountains higher, and the river narrowed as it flowed past the Temple of Horus at Edfu, probably the inspiration for most of the sets for *Aida*. The last stop before Aswan was Kom Ombo, where there was a temple to

Horus the Elder, another form of hawk god, and Sobek, the crocodile god. The Nile was once aswarm with these slithery monsters, and at the turn of the century they were still abundant in Nubia, where they were regularly massacred by tourists; today they are practically extinct.

Aswan was the winter resort par excellence. Here the Nile picked up speed and coursed through black rocks building into a rapids, the emerald green Elephantine Island shone against the rising hills of the desert, and days were spent in reverie over endless cups of sweet mint tea on the terrace of the Cataract Hotel.

The Nubian desert has now disappeared under Lake Nasser, its temples rest under water or in foreign museums, and only the Temple of Abu Simbel has been saved in toto, raised above the waters of the artificial lake. Now, as before, a beam of light reaches into its dark sanctuary in mid-October to mark the anniversary of the reign of Ramses. The golden travelers have disappeared and the dahabiah has been replaced by a quick day trip on a jet plane, but the mystery of ancient Egypt is still with us.

Philae Island, as painted by David Roberts (1796–1864). Philae shared with Abydos the reputation of

being the burial place of Osiris, and was called the Holy Island. None could land on its shores without

permission and a pilgrimage there was the ancient equivalent of a Muslim's voyage to Mecca. During

Greek and Roman rule, the island became the seat of a sacred college and the stronghold of a powerful

hierarchy. Visitors from all over the world came bearing precious gifts. Apparently built by the last of

the native pharaohs, Nectanebo II (BC 361), this is one of the most enchanting sights in all of Egypt.

ACROSS THE POND

Goodbye, On the Mersey by James Tissot,

from the Forbes Magazine Collection,

New York City.

"Say, when does this place get to New York?"
Beatrice Lillie *Across the Pond*

Traversing the Atlantic today is essentially a negative experience that the super-rich, if crossing between New York and London or Paris, choose to shorten with Concorde's supersonic speed. The Concorde is the anesthetic of long-distance travel, a way to arrive fresh and indifferent to one's surroundings, and its exclusivity reflects the class differences and glamour that once existed on the great ocean liners. To ordinary air passengers, crossing eastbound involves a short and sleepless night, the return a grinding and boringly long day.

Until the airplane destroyed the liner, crossing the ocean was often the most sensual and memorable part of a trip abroad. The Atlantic is sublime and mysterious; it can rapidly change mood and color, from glistening blue to gray to white, from somnolent to ferocious. Crisp winds blow over waves that can reach terrifying heights and damage great ships. In the early days,

many small sailing packets and steamers simply disappeared without a trace, victims of storms, icebergs, fires on board, or mechanical catastrophe. And even colossal liners were severely buffeted by waves, which, on occasion, could rise a hundred feet high. As recently as 1966, the Italian Line's 900-foot *Michelangelo* was smashed by a heavy sea that wrecked her bridge, killed three people, and twisted her hull to the point that she was never again able to run at full speed.

The more common curse was seasickness, undramatic but able to reduce the most beautifully decorated ship to a hellhole and the most beautifully dressed passenger to a pathetic wretch eager for death as an alternative. The blessing of Dramamine arrived only after World War II; even so, it—and other medicines—could help only up to a point. Despite such hazards, an Atlantic crossing could be a joy, and so it was to several fortunate generations of travelers who sailed in conditions of comfort and luxury that will never be seen again.

One entered a great liner, like Alice stepping into Wonderland, on a narrow gangplank separating ship

The first-class saloon and stern of HAPAG's *Imperator*, christened in tribute to Germany's Kaiser Wilhelm.

Nicknamed "Limperator" because of her terrible roll, this was the flagship of the line, its interior designed by Mewès

in his famed pseudo-Louis XV style. The great innovation was to divide the boiler uptakes along the side of the

boat—rather than straight through the center—to the funnel, allowing the hundred-foot long lounge (*above*) that

could seat all 700 first-class passengers. The unwieldy eagle (*opposite*) was a gimmick to surpass the length of White

Star's *Olympic*. Its wings were blown off in a storm and thereafter the ugly bird was removed.

from shore. The door was but a small hole in the massive wall of black riveted steel enclosing a self-contained world that would be home for the next five days. First-class passengers were greeted by impeccably dressed stewards who took them down grand staircases or into elevators to deliciously comfortable cabins or suites that had often been booked months in advance.

The choice of ship was not taken lightly, and the lines competed fiercely. Destination, quality of service, beauty, comfort, speed, seaworthiness, cuisine, the captain's personality or fame, the ship's age, and its national affiliation were only some of the elements that influenced passengers to pick the *Mauretania* over the *Imperator*, the *Ile de France* over the *Queen Mary*. Loyalty to a particular ship was important, and regular passengers forged bonds with stewards, who were seldom moved from one liner to another by the company. The barmen never had to ask regulars for their orders; a pink gin or whiskey sour turned up automatically as soon as the guest sat down. Fashion was also important, and ordinary mortals were attracted like moths to the brilliant aura of American millionaires, British royals, and lights of the literary world, stage, or film. Lord Duveen and professional gamblers crossed "the pond" to latch on to the accessible rich, and if the Prince of Wales booked a Cunarder, there was never an empty bed. In fact, the first reading matter for most travelers was the passenger list, slipped under every door before the great liner left port.

BON VOYAGE

In their cabins, popular or important passengers would find large vases of flowers and baskets of fruit, candy, jams, and champagne sent by their friends. The young bellboys, their narrow chests shining with polished brass buttons, would bear these along the crowded corridors to the cabins, followed by stewards or longshoremen carrying suitcases and steamer trunks. Gay confusion reigned as trays were brought in, corks popped, and glasses filled for friends who had come to say good-bye. On some midnight crossings from New York, passengers and visitors wore black tie and evening dress and danced until the final gong chased out

Above Passengers embarking on the *Queen Mary* in 1938. This was the magic moment when ticket-holders

crossed on a gangplank from the real world into the luxurious palace that was to be their home for the next

five days. *Opposite* The Cunard Line *Lusitania* arrives in the New York harbor in September 1907, after her

maiden crossing of the Atlantic. On May 7, 1914, she was sunk off the Irish coast by a German U-boat with a

loss of 1,198 lives including 124 United States citizens.

the last interloper. "All's ashore that's going ashore," shouted the bellboys on the British ships; "*La nave é in partenza. Di sheep is living*," announced the stewards on the Italian Line. Through the cool night air, penetrating the spaces between the tight skyscrapers of the world's greatest port, the ship let out a sad, deep-throated moan reaching all who wished to know that one of the behemoths of the sea was slowly slipping away. "I heard the *Queen Mary* blow one midnight," wrote E. B. White, "and the sound carried the whole history of departure and longing and loss."

The bon-voyage party was a tradition begun when crossing the ocean was a perilous undertaking. People came to share a last anxious moment, to say adieu in the very likely case that the vessel were eaten by ferocious waves or the traveler succumbed to scurvy or disease. Nothing could have been further from the minds of passengers in the heyday of the Atlantic Ferry, and nothing was further than the truth—most of the time. It should be remembered that in their high times the liners were the *only* way to cross; the roaring great Boeing Stratocruisers, developed from the B-29 heavy bomber, were in the future, as were their interminable flights, prolonged by refueling stops at impossibly dreary Gander, Newfoundland, and Ireland's Shannon Airport, where duty-free shopping was invented. That meant the sailings went on year round. The huge ships looked not so huge once on the bound-

ing main, which bounded viciously in the fall and winter.

In bad weather, some passengers retreated to their cabins for the entire duration of the voyage, praying only to die. Even those immune to mal de mer could be served hard knocks, literally. Experience taught the shipping lines to bolt down most furniture—pianos especially—but passengers were not, and ships' doctors, however expensively educated, found that their most-used skills, after soothing the bilious, was wrapping bruises.

The hazard of weather was amplified by the ships themselves, for some behaved badly. The towering *Kaiser Wilhelm der Grosse* looked her mightiest at anchor, for at sea she was known as "Rolling Billy." The *Normandie*, perhaps with French arrogance, was a "stiff ship" that resisted rolling until the last second, then delivered a nasty snap. The *Queen Mary*'s builders were so convinced of her stability that they fitted no handrails in most of her public spaces, but she proved to be a wallower that "broke crockery like an angry fishwife." More than crockery, actually: on her early voyages she was greeted at her New York pier not only by crowds of friends and relatives but by ambulances as well. Denny-Brown stabilizers were eventually fitted to the *Queen Mary* and other ships,

steadying them nicely but knocking the bottom out of the pierside medical trade.

But in better weather an ocean crossing aroused rather than battered the senses. Anybody fortunate enough to have been on a liner subliminally remembers certain smells, tastes, and tactile experiences. The waxy, antiseptic smell of the Cunarders' corridors, the odor of fresh paint perpetually being applied, the explosive sweetness of a fruitcake served with black English tea, the gentle hands of a deck steward bundling his charges in steamer rugs, the sudden salty gusts as one opened a heavy steel door to walk on a

Above **Tea among the palms on the *Rotterdam*.**

Below **The *Mauretania*.**

sloping deck, the ever-present vibration of the engines, and the white roils of the wake, trailing into infinity. There was the way the sea changed color and mood approaching land. And there was the wonderful sense of space and formality that awakened hidden energy and made everybody feel just a bit taller, better behaved, and more civilized. At its best, an ocean crossing on a legendary liner was a perfect marriage of nature and artifice that created magical moments, encouraged romance, and brought people briefly together until the sharp light of day on shore pulled them apart again.

THE CROSSING

Certain things that shaped life at sea during the early days continued until the 1960s, when the Atlantic Ferry came to an end. Many still survive today on the better cruise ships.

One is breakfast in bed, brought by a smiling steward, although some passengers wandered up to the cavernous dining room. Seldom seen now are dining-room tables with fiddle boards—edges that were raised in bad weather to form a protective barrier between diners and their mobile plates—and the extra-high bathroom doorsill that kept water from sloshing out

Above A first class cabin on the *Queen Mary* clearly demonstrates the ample space made available to passengers willing to pay the price. The sinuous lines of the molding, the ample use of clean and light wood panelling and the hideous slippery satin bedspreads and ugly patterns used for curtains and upholstery were Britain's idea of Art Deco chic. *Left* The dour Canadian shipowner, Samuel Cunard, who founded the legendary line, and was more interested in speed and reliability than luxury. He would certainly have disapproved of the *Mary*'s extravagant use of space.

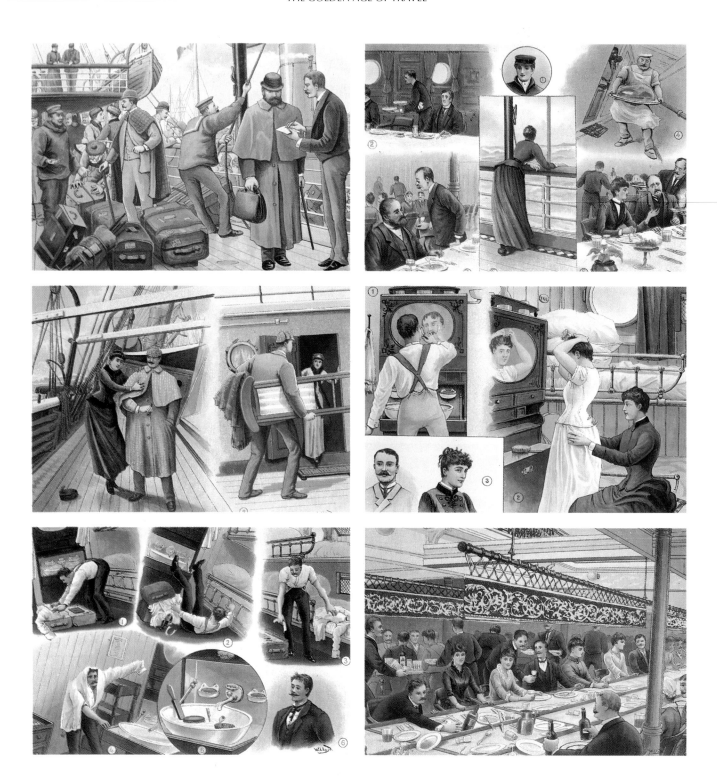

These "P & O Pencillings" came from a book of watercolors and pen-and-ink sketches
made by the illustrator William Whitelock Lloyd. They depict life on board a P&O liner
on the long voyage from London to India c.1890, and the book was sold to passengers as
a memento of their voyage. There was little difference between life on a P&O liner or a
transatlantic crossing until the ship hit the Indian Ocean, when passengers and their
mattresses moved on deck to avoid the

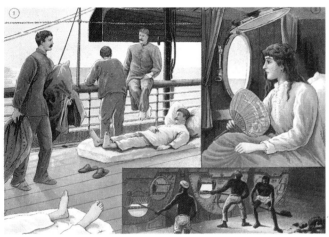

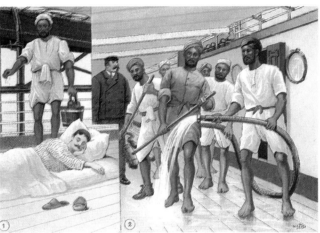

stifling heat (*second row, right hand page*). The ships were
generally filled with somewhat drab British civil servants but a
degree of romance was occasionally introduced by a traveling
maharaja and party. The Maharaja of Jaipur brought aboard large
silver urns of Ganges water for his ablutions, and cast jewels into
the sea before departing in order to assure safe passage.

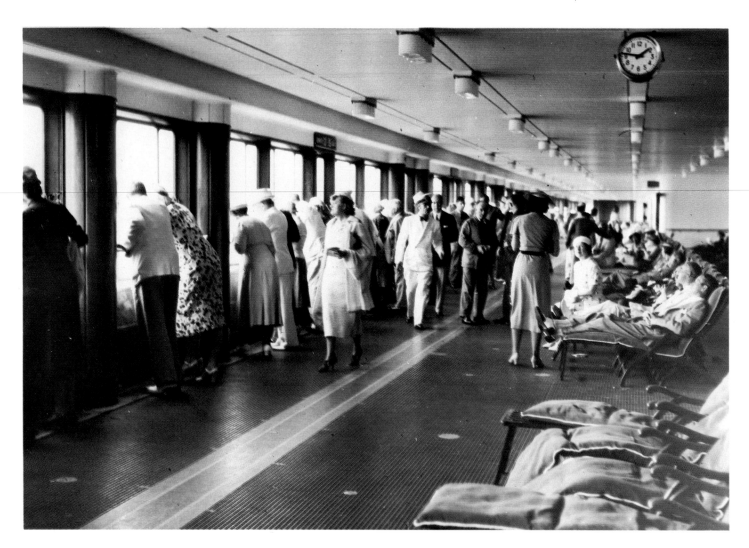

onto the carpet (one learned to stop tripping over it by about the second day), but handrails are still ever-present (even the *Queen Mary* got some eventually).

Mornings at sea were spent walking on deck, playing shuffleboard, or lying on a deck chair with a thick novel and a cup of beef tea. The assignment of deck chairs and dining-room tables was of extreme importance; passengers often would bribe stewards with vast sums of money to be well placed. Ambitious American mothers tried to sit their daughters down in the closest possible proximity to an English lord or an Italian prince; businessmen wanted to rub up against titans of finance and commerce; gamblers sought positions near potential pigeons ripe for plucking over friendly card games; social climbers hawked out chances to meet Mrs. Astor or the Duchess of Marlborough in the conviviality of shipboard life; Lord Duveen wanted to recite his inventory of masterpieces to potential clients. It is no wonder then that the rich and powerful preferred large suites at sea; there they could camp out with family and private servants and be sheltered from latter-day pirates. Privacy, exclusion, and class differences were essential to life on board.

Until the turn of the century, early ships had two

Above and opposite **Two glimpses of deck life on the *Normandie*. This CGT ship used deckspace superbly. Her designers**

cleared away the clutter prevalent on the upper decks of earlier liners, making possible vast, staircase-lined terraces for

walking, outdoor dining, dancing and drinking. Getting a well-placed deck chair, for which there was a supplementary

payment, was the greatest priority after making a table reservation in the dining room. In mid-morning, impeccably dressed

deck stewards passed hot *bouillon* and small sandwiches, and in mid- afternoon placed neat tea-platters on the blanket-

covered laps of their charges. Late at night they pretended to ignore the heavily flirting young women.

Armenians by the Turks, the potato famine in Ireland, and poverty in general drove several generations of the underprivileged, exploited, and persecuted to cross the ocean in search of a future.

The immigrants originally crossed in conditions that were as bad as those they had left in the slums of Liverpool or the shtetls of Lithuania. They were piled one atop the other in wooden bunks, issued an iron plate and spoon, fed gruel twice a day, and had to buy their own straw mattresses, which rapidly became vermin-infested and were thrown overboard before the ship

classes: first, where passengers lived in splendor, and steerage, where squalor reigned. Decks were arranged so that the rich could look down on the poor and be entertained by the dances, songs, and other rituals of Europe's emigrants. On some liners, a notice was posted asking the first-class passengers to desist from throwing food to those in steerage, and stewards discouraged young men, bored by the polite entertainments of their rich parents, from slumming with the livelier steerage crowd. At sea as on land, space was an important class distinction: that is, in steerage there was none. On the *Olympic*, launched in 1911, the room where first-class passengers cooled off after their Turkish bath was half again as large as the third-class galley that cooked meals for a thousand people; it was identical in size to a dormitory that housed forty-two stewards. The supplement charged for a single meal in the *Imperator*'s Ritz-Carlton restaurant equaled the full fare of a passenger in steerage.

STEERAGE

Pampering spoiled passengers brought profits and prestige to the shipping lines, but the real money was made in the immigrant trade. Pogroms of Jews in Russia, Lithuania, and Poland, the wholesale massacre of

In warm weather, life moved to the open deck, as can be seen in these photographs of open-air sports—shuffleboard, fencing, and boxing, taken on cruise ships in the 1930s. Other deck distractions were quoits, tugs of war, and after World War I even tennis on the broad and uncluttered decks of the *Normandie*. The afternoon catch of the ladies, a virtual impossibility at sea, the chic two-toned shoes of one of the pugilists and the high heels of one of the fencers—not to mention the stereotypic good looks of the four shufflers—indicate that these are publicity shots most probably taken in port.

entered New York harbor. Until the mid-nineteenth century, sickness and death traveled in steerage. One line's captains were told to "discourage communications between saloon and steerage passengers, for should it become known to the Health or Quarantine officers that such communication had existed on a voyage in the course of which any contagious or infectious disease had occurred, saloon passengers would probably be made subject to quarantine."

Quarantining first-class passengers would be a financial and public-relations disaster. The term derived from the *quaranta* (forty) days that ships coming from plague ports were isolated in Renaissance Venice; the process was now quicker but still degrading. Ellis Island officials looked immigrants over with hard eyes, seeking signs of tuberculosis, trachoma, and infectious

Above Bathers in the Delft-tiled pool of the Holland

America Line's *Statendam*. *Opposite* Passengers pose in

evening dress on the staircse of HAPAG's *Albert Ballin*, a

small ship named after the manager who brought his line

unparalleled renown thanks to a fanatic attention to detail

and a flair for luxury.

diseases. The unhealthy were turned away, returned to Europe at the shipping lines' expense.

Shipowner William Inman was the first to improve the immigrants' lot. For thirty dollars, he transported them, fed them decently (arrowroot, porridge, and molasses for breakfast; beef for lunch; tea and gruel for supper), and provided bearable if primitive sanitation. The HAPAG line in 1906 created an entire village where immigrants were received, examined, and thoroughly showered in preparation for the crossing. This saved time and trouble later, and word rapidly spread that the German ships offered the best crossing to a new life, including three meals served by stewards. Immigrants otherwise had little to base their decision on, except which ships were the most powerful and,

hence, the safest. Ships with three funnels looked mightier than those with two, and so it was poor, illiterate immigrants who inspired the great *four*-funnel liners. For years liners had more funnels than necessary; one was often a dummy, in some instances used as a kennel for first-class dogs.

The greatest advance for the immigrants was improved medical care, which was inevitable once the lines began treating them as human beings instead of cattle. Pregnant immigrant women often sailed close to their due dates in the hope of giving birth aboard. The delivery was free and the treatment far better than the poor received ashore. When that occurred, the ship would be officially commemorated: should you chance to meet someone with, say, *Berengaria* somewhere in her name, you may reasonably conclude that she or an ancestor was of immigrant stock, born at sea between the Old World and the New.

KEEPING BUSY ON BOARD

Official separation between classes was paralleled in part by separation of the sexes. The smoking room and bar were very much the enclave of gentlemen, the winter garden and reading room were for the ladies. If any of the single ladies aboard wanted to meet the single men, they had little chance to do so over dinner, as head stewards would round them up and assign them to a girl-ghetto table. Shipboard romances did blossom nevertheless, but without the shipping line playing cupid —in the brief span of a crossing, a fling was sometimes just another thing to do, or at least hope to do.

Apart from that there were endless games of bridge, whist, poker, and gin rummy—players occasionally stopped to sleep, but the more obsessed skipped dinner and had sandwiches brought to the card table. When the *Titanic* hit the famous iceberg, and its passengers were coaxed out on deck in their life jackets, several gents remained fixed to their leather chairs dealing out the cards. There were horse races in the evening, with wooden nags moved along felt courses according to the roll of the dice; there were also bingo and betting on the ship's pool, based on how many miles she would travel on a particular day. Large bets

Two magnificent photographs by Lewis Hine (*above*) and Alfred Stieglitz (*opposite*) taken respectively in 1905 and 1911, perfectly summarize the depressing conditions of travel for European emigrants in the early years of this century. Even though by this time life at sea had improved considerably, the contrast between rich and poor was seldom more marked than on a sea crossing aboard a transatlantic liner. Liners, in fact, made far more money transporting the poor than the rich, and competed strongly for their business. After the depression of 1929, when this traffic diminished, the lines were forced to transform large areas devoted to steerage passengers into "tourist class" for students and middle-class passengers and even for emigrants who had saved up for a visit to their relatives.

were also made on everything from tugs-of-war to boxing matches between members of the crew. Other activities were shuffleboard, quoits, ping-pong, skeet-shooting, squash, deck tennis, brisk walks on deck, driving golf balls off the stern, swimming in the pools (indoor and out), and riding the exercycles and electric horses and camels in the gymnasium (the high prelate who fell from one of these aboard a Cunarder achieved the unique distinction of being the only archbishop of Canterbury to be thrown from a horse in mid-ocean).

The sedentary enjoyed concerts, amateur theatricals, movies, and absolutely nonstop eating and drinking. Breakfast spilled into 11:00 A.M. bouillon on deck, and then drinks in all the bars, saloons, and smoking rooms preceded a large lunch. By mid-afternoon, the tables were laid for tea, which was also carried around to the deck chairs. There was a short rest before the change into evening clothes to hit the bars and lounges once more for long drinks before dinner. Then there was talking and dancing into the early hours, followed by another visit to a large buffet to settle the stomach for sleep.

There were several gastronomic shipboard traditions in first class. One was that the menu always had to be honored; if among ten main courses everybody chose Sole Florentine, face could not be lost by turning down a single request. Another tradition was that a chef could cook anything requested by passengers of a mind to test him with the most incredible and exotic dishes. There was no Fortnum & Mason on the high

seas, so the provisions stocked had to be staggering in variety and quantity. Caviar at dinner was de rigueur, and it was served without limit. Bread was baked daily; whatever was uneaten was thrown overboard. The waste was appalling, but the finest leftovers, at least, were always sent down to the stokers, or the "black gang," as consolation for their back-breaking work.

Dressing was ritualized. Evening dress was required except for the first and last nights, so the giant steamer trunks could be packed and unpacked. Tweeds were preferred by both ladies and gentlemen through lunch, and men generally wore matching caps and knickers. Ladies usually changed for tea into something diaphanous and seductive. The best evening dresses and jewels were kept for the captain's dinner, on the next-to-last night. Its menu was particularly elaborate, and gentlemen at the captain's table often wore white tie and decorations. There followed a benefit for seamen's charities that displayed the varied talents of the passengers. One wonders who could possibly have dreamed up some of the programs. Mischa Elman or Jascha Heifetz would be followed by a ventriloquist or a piano teacher from Manchester; Paderewski by an amateur magician pulling rabbits out of a hat. Once the *Ile de France*'s captain stopped the ship and poured oil on the water so the great Pavlova could perform the death of the swan without risking injury. Another night

Above Watching the movies in the salon of

HAPAG's *New York. Below* Tea-time on board the

Cap Arcona in 1927. Indoor life, particularly in

calm seas, was a gentle round of agreeable

entertainments from breakfast in bed to dancing

after midnight.

aboard was usually devoted to a costume ball; passengers disguised or decorated themselves with whatever they could find (often with the help of clever stewards) in the hope of winning a prize.

SHIPBOARD ROMANCE

The glamour of the crossing, combined with being cut off from the rest of the world with nothing useful to do, was an ideal stimulant to the libido, particularly after World War I, when a younger generation began traveling for pleasure and adventure. Shipboard romance was a staple of films, novels, and theater, and many passengers crossed in bed rather than on deck. Some who met aboard fell in love; others married ashore and went aboard as an alternative to Niagara Falls. Even before crossing the gangplank young men scouted the boat train or the *gare maritime* to appraise the romantic potential of the voyage.

C. W. R. Winter, who served many years on the *Queen Mary*, wrote of finding couples locked together late at night in various states of dishevelment in the lounges, in lifeboats, and on deck chairs, and in a charming vignette describes how the ship's switchboard would suddenly light up ten minutes after the dancing in the veranda grill had ended. In those days of better manners and more discreet sex, the boys would return to their cabins before proposing a shared night to the girls. As single people were often bunked with strangers, sleeping arrangements could get complicated, and accommodating an amorous roommate was a source of either amusement or annoyance. Ideally, two boys in one cabin would pine after two girls in another. Often, however, a flapper would be roomed with a dowager and a college sophomore with a geriatric case. The only solution then was love in the afternoon, otherwise known as "taking to the boats."

The arbitrary placement of strangers in a cabin was potentially explosive. Passengers argued about closet space, toilet habits, neatness, smoking, snoring, and late hours, and there were occasions when one

Dancing on the *Imperator* in 1914. The white tie and tails of the gentlemen and long dresses of the ladies indicate that this was the evening of the captain's dinner, the most elegant event of the transatlantic crossing. The same would hold true for the fashion plate (*left*), on Devambez's CGT poster, although top hats were not *de rigeur* even for the last night out. The enormous main salon of the German ship was converted every evening into a splendid ballroom.

passenger proposed the customs of ancient Greece to a horrified roommate. Right after World War II, when space on liners was at a premium, my mother shared a cabin on the *Queen Elizabeth* with an unbearably rude and messy woman. Life was highly unpleasant until her cabinmate saw her dining with Cary Grant and Marlene Dietrich. That very night the cabin became impeccable and the bathroom spotless; mother's night-gown had been laid out, the sheets were turned down, and the tigress became a pussycat.

Romance at sea also had its professional side. Cour-tesans—they were too fancy to be called prostitutes —regularly plied their trade afloat. They were, in gen-eral, distinguishable from legitimate ladies by their bet-ter looks, superior figures, fancier clothes, and finer jewelry. As their clients tended to show loyalty toward a given ship, they avoided embarrassment by regularly changing liners, coming to New York on the *Bremen* or the *Queen Mary* and, after a few days of shopping, returning on the *Normandie* or the *Conte di Savoia*. A traditional transatlantic scam was to lure a gentleman into bed and then have a furious "husband" charge in, fired with the kind of outrage only blackmail could assuage. When such scandals were uncovered, they were usually squelched by one of the ship's officers, who were constantly on the lookout.

The large cast of floating card sharks posed similar problems. One ship's captain was known, after being tipped off by the purser or chief steward, to interview

sharp dealers in his cabin. The two would have a brief but friendly chat, the captain on his side of his desk, the miscreant on the other, and the captain's enormous pistol in the middle. A ship's officer would always have a warning word with any shady character he recognized on sight, but otherwise nothing *could* be done until something *had* been done: there was no way to stop a villain from booking passage.

THE BLUE RIBAND

The continuing battle for prestige on the Atlantic was most excitingly expressed in the Blue Riband, symbol of the fastest crossing by a liner between England's Bishop Rock and New York's Ambrose Light—2,907 miles. No blue riband actually existed, nor was there any prize-giving body to award it. Once a liner captured the title it was a foregone conclusion that she would never steam as fast again: the cost in excess fuel consumption was astronomical, and such a turn of speed was not only unnecessary but really of little use. Continued high-speed running by one ship in the line would upset the carefully balanced schedule of the others.

Finally, for all the time, treasure, and effort spent on capturing the speed championship of the Atlantic, no one ever admitted to seeking it. However, it involved the honor and pride of great nations, especially

Above An artist's rendition of satiated first-class passengers after a delicious CGT dinner on

board the small and lovely Art Deco *Mariette Pasha* in 1926. *Below* A concert program on

North German Lloyd's *Bremen*. Concerts often followed dinner, and a string ensemble always

played at tea-time on board a luxury liner. The CGT was particularly famous for its food, which

equaled and sometimes even surpassed that of the best restaurants of Paris. The French line was

also the most fun, particularly between the wars on the *Paris, France* and *Normandie*.

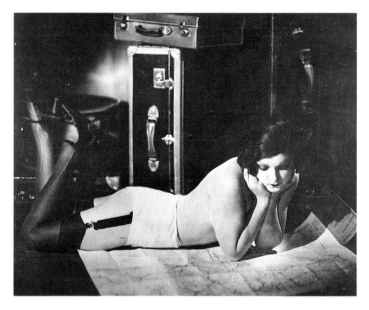

gineer set a number that dictated the black gang's work. A setting of seven meant that they had seven minutes to cut the soft coal, rake out the grates, and shovel in a new load of fuel before the bell rang and they had to repeat the operation. Bare-chested and streaming with sweat, the stokers' skin burned from the flames. Despite heavy gloves, their hands were a mass of blisters; their feet were seared despite the high wooden clogs worn to protect against the ashes and embers littering the deck. They grew deaf and deranged from the incredible din of whirling machinery.

The lower the number, the harder the work and the greater the danger. When the ship rolled and pitched in high seas, red-hot coals spilled out of the grates; when the fires became infernos the draft was so powerful that a man who lost his footing might literally be sucked into the furnace. The reprieve that came when

Germany and Britain, which passed the prize back and forth between them. The French held it briefly with their magnificent *Normandie*, the Italians once with the *Rex*, and the United States had two Atlantic champions. The second and more famous one was the wonderful *United States*, which crossed in a miraculous three days, ten hours, and forty minutes in 1952. The *United States* steamed so fast that she beat the *Queen Mary*'s time by ten hours and, like a real thoroughbred, cleaved the waves so muscularly that she stripped the paint off her waterline. She actually could have done better, but because of her military potential as a troopship, the government wanted her top speed kept secret. Retired since the Atlantic Ferry ended two decades ago, she still holds the Blue Riband, and no contender is in sight.

The cost of winning—and defending—the title was colossal. When the average speed of a liner at the turn of the century was twenty knots, every *additional* knot cost as much as the first twenty. The victims of Blue Riband racing, however, were not the bean-counters in the head office but the black gangs, or stokers, who shoveled endless tons of coal to feed the fires beneath the boilers. Stokers were always poor and often illiterate men, greatly given to drink and fighting but desperate and brawny enough to labor like demons in the pit. When the captain rang down for speed, the chief en-

Romance was one of the main activities for the young on shipboard, although this girl (*above*) looks as if she has just been jilted. The amorous couple (*right*), on deck in this 1920s magazine illustration, seem to have aroused the indignation of an older passenger—or perhaps he is simply jealous. Ships' doctors and chief pursers were generally prepared for the advances of amorous ladies, but one might wonder about the intentions of the old Cunard deckhand (*left*), in Curr's 1925 poster entitled "Atlantic Summer Holidays."

the number was raised might only mean more misery later, when the ship had to make up for lost time.

The barbarity of the stokeholds was not solely a product of racing for the Blue Riband; it existed, in fact, on every express liner that made money with fast passages on schedule. Not until fuel oil replaced coal did such slavery pass and liner life downstairs become even remotely as civilized as upstairs. But that perhaps meant only that the stoker's lot was even worse: now he was unemployed.

The Blue Riband was often won on a ship's maiden voyage. Thus, the maiden sailings of new contenders attracted, in addition to the usual run of passengers, others whose special thrill was being in on a big event, like a space launch or the Concorde's first flight. And since everybody knew what was up, the excitement was almost palpable and the ship's pool reached incredible sums. Shouts of joy rang over the waters as the new champion's prow cut through the calm waters at Ambrose Light, passengers linked hands to waists to dance in conga lines around the decks, and champagne flowed as history was made.

FEEDING THE MONSTER
Even before a ship made port, preparations began for the turnaround—schedules had to be maintained, and ships tied to piers paid huge port fees instead of earning revenue. Mountains of dirty linens were prepared

for delivery to the laundry, inventories were taken, and water ballast was emptied out of fuel tanks. Even as passengers disembarked, lines of trucks gathered at the pier with replenishments, and in home port the line's executives arrived with long lists or bureaucratic documents, and workmen boarded to make any necessary repairs. Provisioning was a complicated matter and publicity officers adored providing the newspapers with impressive details on the food, liquor, and supplies needed for a crossing.

Due to their transatlantic character, a liner's shopping was international. Idaho potatoes generally won out over Europe's waxier spuds; Maine lobsters were preferred to Brittany's; Dover sole to Long Island's flounder. Cheeses and wines came from France; barrels of caviar were loaded on both sides of the Atlantic, and so were sides of beef (some preferred American steaks to France's *entrecôtes*). There were Scotch pheasants, Smithfield hams, and tons of fresh vegetables.

Refueling became easy when oil came in, but before oil there was the nightmare of "coaling up." A medium-size liner of 30,000 tons would burn three hundred carloads of coal during a crossing. When a ship was "coaled," filthy black dust was everywhere. Portholes and doors were sealed, stewards covered the furniture, and the entire vessel had to be swabbed down afterward. Most of the crew had to remain aboard or on the pier to assist in the turnaround, although the stokers generally vented their frustrations in great bouts of drinking and fighting in the waterfront bars: those not clapped in jail often were carried back in wheelbarrows. The crews led lives of incredible sacrifice, coming home only a few times a year to their wives and children, working odd hours, sleeping in cramped quarters, and largely living off tips.

SERVICE
Speed, technical innovation, and glamorous decoration were important in the making of a great liner, but in the end it was service that counted because it was service that passengers remembered. It was an art handed down in a strict hierarchy, from the captain to the deckhands.

A liner's captain needed a wealth of technical know-

Opposite The *Bremen*, cheered on her arrival in New York in July 1929 after snatching the Blue Riband from the *Mauretania* which had kept it for 22 years. The time logged was 4 days and 17 hours, and victory was particularly sweet after Germany's defeat and humiliation in World War I. The tug boat *Macon* carried a band as well as Police Commissioner Grover Whalen. *Above* The *Normandie*, which also took the Blue Riband on her maiden voyage on June 3, 1935 at an average speed of 29.6 knots, covering the course in 4 days, 3 hours and 2 minutes. The crew and passengers were so sure of victory that most of the passengers dressed in blue the night before arrival, or at least wore blue scarves.

Captains were totally attached to their ships. Sir James Charles died as he docked the *Berengaria* at Southampton, and Sir James Netley died in his cabin aboard the *Aquitania* between Cherbourg and Southampton. Both knew that they were on their last crossing before obligatory retirement, and they died, it was generally felt, of broken hearts.

Most of a ship's hierarchy was of little interest to the passengers. They knew the captain was all-powerful —"master before God" is the official description of a captain's license or "ticket"—and would have committed crimes of violence to dine at his table. The chief steward was in effect a hotel manager, and it was always well to be in good standing with somebody who controlled seating assignments at dinner. The purser was a sort of social arbiter; he assigned cabins, organized entertainment, supervised the arrival and departure of passengers, stored their jewelry, listened to complaints, and played genial host to a shipful of sometimes difficult people. A "happy ship" depended much on him.

The most famous and beloved purser of all was Henri Villar, of the *Ile de France* and the *Normandie*. He brought to his liners all the elegance, fun, and refinement of Paris; he also had an encyclopedic knowledge of the social, political, and business worlds of several nations. It was once reported that on one liner a famous politician was inadvertently seated at dinner with his ex-wife's corespondent, but that did not happen on a Villar ship.

The British offered probably the best all-around service, the Americans the worst. Devoted Cunard and White Star workers knew their place and combined civility, friendliness, and respect in a most extraordinary way. This was the product of a hierarchal society that had not been rocked by revolution, by an underlying concern for one's fellow man, and by the naval discipline that prevailed. The French could not quite find the correct balance between servility and self-respect, the Germans were too stiff and rigid, and the Yankees were not about to take any nonsense from anybody. Their ancestors had not crossed the ocean in steerage for them to be subservient to the rich or titled. As for the Italians, they were always the first to rush for the lifeboats in case of danger.

ledge, experience, a capacity for leadership, and social flair. The skippers of the Cunard flagships were called commodores, and were knighted by their sovereign for long and faithful service. All captains had to be skillful at charming the wife of a head of state or a society queen; they had to preside as authoritatively over Divine Service as they did on the bridge. Cunard-White Star once proclaimed that "All of our twenty-four captains are officers in the Royal Navy Reserve. Twenty-two have the Royal Decoration. Six are Officers of the Order of the British Empire. Two have the Distinguished Service Cross. One is a Baronet. One is Aide de Camp to His Majesty King Edward VIII. . .an honour, the highest that can be conferred, granted to one only in the merchant service."

Above **The control board area of the engine room of the *Normandie* was dramatically different from that of earlier coal-burning liners. Diesel fuel was far easier to handle and load than the mountains of coal that once had to be shovelled day and night by a crew of stokers known as "the black gang." The *Normandie*'s power plant, which propelled the ship and provided electricity for its lights, air-conditioning, elevators, and everything else needed to provide the passengers' comfort, supplied enough electricity to run a large city such as Boston. The *Normandie*'s engines were run by turbo-electric propulsion, a total innovation for a great liner.**

THE AMERICAN LINES

The United States made a short but particularly brilliant foray into the transatlantic arena with the Collins Line, starting in the late 1840s and ending in 1858. Edward Knight Collins wrested the Blue Riband from Cunard, produced a series of ships of great magnificence, and reigned supreme on the high seas for several years. Collins came from a renowned family of New England sea captains and had made a small fortune in freight-carrying packets. He then built a group of vessels named after great actors—*Garrick*, *Siddons*, *Sheridan*, and *Roscius*—which became known as "The Dramatic Line." Each ship had an effigy of its particular thespian, and, in contrast to the conservative and staid Cunarders, was decorated in an entertaining and theatrical style.

Cunard's virtual dominance of the transatlantic mail annoyed the United States Congress. Independence, after all, was already half a century behind the young nation. Collins lobbied for a subsidy large enough to give Cunard a run for its money, and his qualifications and past success with both freight and passengers convinced his government that he was their man. Collins's firing shot was two splendid wooden liners, rather obviously christened *Atlantic* and *Pacific*, each 282 feet long and weighing 2,856 tons, and both launched on February 1, 1849. These paddle steamers had comforts never before seen on a liner—steam heating, ice in the galleys to keep produce fresh, even a barbershop. The dining room was sixty-seven feet by twenty feet, and the Collins brochures gushed in the usual way about the splendid appointments of these new conquerors of the sea. The *Atlantic* also had the first oceangoing smoking room, an appurtenance that quickly became standard in all liners, and the only complaint from passengers concerned the ship's tiny staterooms. After a shaky start, she paddled back from Liverpool to New York in a record ten days and sixteen hours. These ships were followed by the building of the equaly splendid Collins liners, *Arctic* and *Baltic*. The transatlantic race quickly became a family game among these four ships, which not only guaranteed speed but also comfort of a sort unmatched by any other liners. In 1854 Collins met his first great setback when the *Arctic* sank with a loss of 322 lives, including those of his wife, son, and daughter.

Above left Workers in the "garde manger" of the *Paris* inspect and store vegetables prior to the ship's crossing. Produce was bought throughout the world under the supervision of the head steward and *chef de cuisine. Above* Laundresses at work on the SS *Caledonia*. Passengers' clothes were pressed and their laundry washed and ironed for a supplement. Sheets and towels were generally handled on land.

A ship was really a gigantic travelling hotel, and the Chief Steward was essentially a hotel manager responsible for a large crew that supplied the comforts of his spoiled passengers.

The rankled Cunard Line launched the steel-hulled *Persia* to recapture its reputation for speed. In January 1856, the *Persia* raced across the iceberg-filled North Atlantic in a furious attempt to beat the *Pacific*'s nine-day record and quickly hit an iceberg. The *Pacific* had preceded her across the Atlantic at full speed, fully aware of Cunard's intentions. The *Persia*, a battered survivor thanks to her steel hull, was towed into New York; no trace of the *Pacific* was found. She had been lost at sea in one of the period's most publicized shipwrecks. The government and the bankers began to think that financing disasters was poor policy and they started to withdraw their backing, just as Collins was building his largest and finest ship, the 3,670-ton *Adriatic*. The liner hardly sailed under Collins's flag, and when his *Baltic* berthed on February 18, 1857, the game was over. The three great ships—*Adriatic*, *Baltic*, and *Atlantic*—were auctioned for a piddling $50,000.

WAR

World War I started much earlier for Europe than for the United States, which was kept out of its early stages by the isolationist sentiment of its people and the formidable barrier of the Atlantic Ocean, over which some liners briefly continued to run despite the hostilities. On July 31, 1914, the captain of the *Kronprinzessin Cecilie* received a coded message that hostilities were about to break out and that he should take every possible precaution to avoid being captured by the British, since the hold of his ship was filled with bullion on its way back to the imperial vaults. In this gentler world, the captain headed towards Maine's Bar Harbor, into which he was guided by one of the resort's elegant yachtsmen. Captain Palack and his crew became the hit of the social season, their band played on the village green, and local businesses gave dinner parties in their honor.

While many liners were sunk in the great conflict,

This numbered cross-section of the 1,029ft., 79,280-ton *Normandie* gives an idea of the facilities of the world's most luxurious liner. Among other noteworthy features are, by numbers on the diagram, Sun deck: 3, 4, Luxury suite and private terrace. Embarkation deck: 21, Café grill room with dance floor. Promenade deck: 34, Terrace or veranda cabins, 36–41, Grand staircase, First class smoking room, Grand lounge, Gallery lounge, Upper hall and elevators, Theater, 46, Winter garden with giant bronze bird cages. Main deck: 55, Tourist class reading room, 56, Tourist class lounge, 71, Hairdressing salon. B deck: 113–117, Medical center.

it was the torpedoing of the *Lusitania* that had the greatest effect. She was, after all, the sister ship of the legendary *Mauretania*, and was carrying 124 United States citizens when she approached the Old Head of Kinsale off the Irish coast on May 7, 1915.

The captain had been given instructions to zigzag in order to avoid the far slower U-boats, but understood the instructions to mean that he should adopt these measures only once a U-boat had been sighted. Submarines had been seen off the coast for some time, and the *Lusitania* headed into the view of Commander Walther Schweiger's periscope. He had only one torpedo left, and it silently headed straight for the midship section of the long, elegant liner. It was a perfect hit, and the explosion exceeded all possible expectations. Although there has never been official confirmation, it is quite likely that the ship was secretly carrying tons of explosives from the United States to Great Britain. Consequently, the ship sank quickly, the lifeboats were practically useless, and, despite the nearness of the coast and the warm summer waters, 1,198 lives were lost out of a total of 1,254 passengers and 850 crew.

C desk: 127, First class dining room, 129, Chapel. D deck: 141–150, Kitchens and food

storage, 154, Exercise room, 155, 156, Swiming pool and bar, 159, Automobile

embarkation and elevators. F deck: 173–175, Laundry, 176—179, Cold storage, 180,

Baggage hold, 181, Garage. Bottom: 186, Propeller shafts, 187, Compartment for 4

electric motors, 189, Compartment for turbo- alternators and auxiliaries, 190, Boilers.

Above A bell boy delivering a telegram on the promenade deck of the *Ile de France*.

THE BIRTH OF THE MODERN LINER

The *Queen Mary*, docked in Southampton, 1903.

This legendary Cunarder, along with the

Normandie, was conceived and built during the

Great Depression and symbolized hope for a

brighter future.

The war marked the end of the Belle Epoque. The flower of Europe's youth lay trampled in the trenches, imperial Russia had been shattered by a bloody revolution, the kaiser was in exile in Holland, and twilight was setting on the Hapsburg Empire. The waltz was being replaced by the Charleston, and for the first time a devastated Europe looked to the United States for leadership. Woodrow Wilson dictated his fourteen points at the Versailles conference, and the victorious allies imposed impossible reparations on a defeated Germany, sowing the seeds of a conflict far more devastating than the horror that had just transpired.

All this meant a flow of business toward the victorious, unscathed United States. As Wall Street boomed for a decade after the end of hostilities, an unprecedented number of new luxury hotels were put up in New York City to accommodate the stream of visitors. Among the most outstanding were the Ambassador, the giant Roosevelt (with 1,100 rooms), the Drake, Barclay, Park Lane, Ritz Towers, Sherry Netherland, Governor Clinton, St. Moritz, Essex House, and Hampshire House. The magnificent new Waldorf-Astoria had its own train station for private railroad cars, its luxurious towers, and splendid Art Deco decoration. Planned throughout the giddy 1920s, some of these hotels were finished in the depressed years of the thirties and had trouble surviving.

A great change on the Atlantic in these years was the new planning of space. When the United States instituted a quota on immigration, vast parts of the ships previously devoted to steerage were suddenly empty. The solution was to create two new classes, "cabin" and "tourist," the latter referred to in liner publicity as "the left-bank class," in deference to the fun life sought out by the young on a budget of a few dollars a day at a time when a buck stretched quite far.

The old German ships were now sailing under new flags. The *Imperator* became the Cunard *Berengaria*, and her famous Ritz-Carlton restaurant was converted into a ballroom. The new owners did not even bother to change the taps from "*auf*" and "*zu*" to "open" and "closed." The other captured liners rusted together in Chesapeake Bay. The *Mauretania* went back into service for Cunard, as did the *Aquitania*.

VIVE LA FRANCE!

The interwar period witnessed the rise of the French Line, the Compagnie Générale Transatlantique (CGT). The CGT had built the *France* just before the war. It epitomized the Gallic sense of grandeur, as if the CGT intended it to sail with Louis XIV, Louis XV, Madame de Pompadour, and Marie Antoinette on board. It quickly became known as "the Château of the Atlantic." Everything was curved, gilded, and watched over by portraits of the Sun King and his favorites at Versailles. The embarkation hall's staircase was copied after the one in the Bibliothèque Nationale, and France's colonies were acknowledged by a *Salon Mauresque*, in which pantalooned blackamoors poured coffee after dinner. For the first time on the Atlantic, the dining

Above Imperator leaving Hamburg on her maiden voyage. *Opposite* The North German

Lloyd *Europe* and *Bremen*, sister ships and superstars of the line, flank the *Columbus* in

this beautifully designed poster that emphasizes the strength and speed of the low slung

liners. They were designed to snatch the Blue Riband and make a nationalistic statement

of Germany's ability to come back from the devastation of World War I and the

humiliation of the Treaty of Versailles.

room was entered by a great staircase that permitted the ladies to make a splendid entrance on their way to dinner. This was a feature of French liners; the British simply walked up to their supper table. The French are great people watchers, and the *grande descente* was the rich man's equivalent of the sidewalk café, a wonderful vehicle for displaying the magnificent dresses of Patou, Lanvin, and Poiret, as well as a good way to see who was on board. And once the chic passengers sat down, they were served the best food on the Atlantic.

The *Paris* went into service in 1921 and was the most profitable ship on the Atlantic. She was not as pretentious as the *France*, and made a serious attempt to look at her own time, not just at the past. She was a bridge between the ship as a somewhat ridiculous floating museum and the ship as an expression of contemporary taste and sensibility; she perfectly reflected the passing of an old, established society. The *Paris* totally cast off the past in 1929 when, after a fire, her public rooms were remodeled in the taste of the 1925 *Exposition Internationale des Arts Décoratifs*.

This legendary and trend-setting exposition dictated the decoration of the *Ile de France*, which was the first ship ever to *totally* reflect the taste of her time. John dal Piaz, the brilliant president of the CGT, decided that "Living isn't copying, it's creating." This revolutionized the design of liners. Built in 1927, the *Ile* was a ship for flappers, modern yet comfortable, stylish and fun even though an excess of glass and marble inspired by the 1925 exhibition conveyed a certain coldness. Its grand suite was sublime. It contained a drawing room and dining room divided by modernist iron gates, three bedrooms, and sunken baths. The *Paris, France,* and *Ile de France* quickly gained reputations as the best transatlantic liners. They were smaller than the German, American, and British dinosaurs and in many ways not as seaworthy, but they had style.

A NEW WORLD

The French ships reflected the postwar years, when accidents of birth gave way to talent. The old aristocracy was on the wane. In Paris, Russian nobles were driving taxis, Prince Yussupov was selling dresses, and the Grand Duke Mikhail was chasing Coco Chanel. In Germany and Austria, a decimated aristocracy had difficulty making ends meet. Hollywood was on the rise and the new kings and queens were building palaces in Beverly Hills. Charlie Chaplin, Douglas Fairbanks, and Mary Pickford were the heroes of the day and the center of attention on the great liners. Established society had given way to café society, epitomized in a new and skinny heir to the throne who flaunted convention and whiled away his evenings at the Ambassador, where one could "dance with the man who danced with the girl who danced with the Prince of Wales." F. Scott Fitzgerald's Nick and Nicole Diver represented the lost generation, the emptiness of the expatriate Americans who were searching for themselves abroad. In the United States, the Volstead Act of 1919 brought in prohibition, which drove steady drinkers across the seas. Many of them had to be carried out of the bars of the liners.

In the twenties, Wall Street boomed on easy credit and there prosperity seemed endless. Taxi drivers and chauffeurs borrowed money to play the hot tips they heard their customers discussing, giant mansions were built, Rolls-Royces were ordered, and euphoria ran high. These years marked the last great expansive wave of the golden age of travel as new liners were commissioned, many completed just as or shortly after the Depression hit. Germany was the first to rise to the occasion with new and powerful ships. The *Bremen* and *Europa* were launched within a day of each other in August 1928. Both were wonders of design, with sleek lines and two rakish mustard funnels. They lay low in the water and sailed through the Atlantic with a businesslike fury, as if eager to prove that *Deutschland* was still *über alles*. These were not majestic floating palaces; they were streamlined bullies that immediately snatched the Blue Riband from the *Mauretania* on the *Bremen*'s maiden voyage in July 1929, cutting an amazing ten hours off the existing record. When the *Europa* sailed in March 1930, she beat that record by another eighteen minutes, and the ships carried 12 percent of all transatlantic passengers. Like the *Ile de France*, their decoration was modern and of a whole. "The ostentatious luxury of former times...has been avoided by laying stress on the beauty of line and on the superior quality of materials. The architecture of

the *Bremen* emancipates us from a time which is not our own and leads us into the grandeur of the present age,'' wrote their Düsseldorf architect, Fritz August Breuhaus de Groot. His simple, economic lines, unadorned surfaces, Bauhaus furniture, and lack of frills created an atmosphere of severity and coldness.

VIVA ITALIA!

Italian shipping lines were not interested in forgetting ''the ostentatious luxury of former times.'' Starting in 1922 and 1923 with the small *Conte Rosso* and *Conte Verde*, they made an astonishing *retardataire* splash thanks to a design firm, La Casa Artistica, in Florence, Trieste, and Genoa, a creation of the incredibly gifted

Coppedès whose clients included J. P. Morgan, the Rothschilds, and the Italian royal family. The Coppedès created a hodgepodge of historic periods glued together with gilded stucco, much like the extravagant movie palaces of the period. There was never a plain surface to rest the eye, even on the ceilings, as bits of ancient Rome and Granada collided with the then-fashionable *stile Liberty*, as the Art Nouveau style was called in Italy. It was as if several opera sets had been pulled out simultaneously by a confused stage crew. Curiously, the formula worked and the Italian Line became a major presence and—along with the CGT and North German Lloyd—gave the staid British a run for their money. The last of the *Contes* was a seagoing palazzo, the *Conte di Savoia* of 1931, whose vast main lounge was vaulted by a faithfully painted recreation of the ceiling in the Palazzo Colonna. The floors of the great *galleria* were in linoleum, and the modern sofas upholstered in imitation zebra skin. Her sister ship, the *Rex*, briefly held the Blue Riband.

There was a great amount of activity on the South Atlantic, particularly between Naples and Genoa and South America, which drew many Italian immigrants to the potential riches of Argentina's pampas and the rich jungles of Brazil. This southern route promised not only calm seas but bright sunshine, and the lifestyle en route was very different from that on the cold Atlantic. The *Saturnia* and *Vulcania* of 1927 were full of light wicker furniture, and many staterooms had enchanting, trellis-lined private terraces on which to enjoy the sunshine. These liners were also decorated by the theatrical Coppedès, and both ships had identical Louis XIV ballrooms. They also had indoor pools that were a dazzling reflection of ancient Pompeii and the first large outdoor pools to be built onto a giant liner's deck. These Italian confections were the last floating echoes of the past, and they set the style for the cruise ship that today is one of the last remnants of the golden age of travel.

THE GREAT DEPRESSION

As the new liners and hotels that were built on a wave of optimism went into operation or reached

This poster signed Riccobaldi (1927)

glorifies the liners of the Italian company, Lloyd Sabaudo,

and shows typical futurist inspiration.

completion, the first cracks started to appear in the credit-based financial structure invented by the geniuses of Wall Street. On October 30, 1929, the house of cards came tumbling down. In a few hours, as stock prices headed toward the basement, paper millionaires became paupers. Speculators flew out of windows in suicide leaps, and many passengers on eastbound liners were constrained from diving overboard. The once-rich, traveling around Europe with servants and families, crowded the offices of the shipping lines in Paris and London to get a quick ticket back home to assess the damage.

J. P. Morgan was no longer alive to save the day, as he had done in the past, single-handedly stemming panics. The financial world crumbled, America's great industries faltered, unemployment soared, and governments sought protection by putting up walls of protective tariffs that deepened the crisis even further. The Great Depression, however, did not spell the end of luxury travel. The very rich were still rich, and everything now cost much less. Not everybody had invested all their money in the stock market, and there were even a few short sellers who had cleaned up on the misfortune of the eternal optimists. Hollywood's stars made fortunes as more and more people sought escape in the dark rooms of the movie palaces, obedient subjects still paid their tithes to maharajas, and financiers borrowed deutschemarks to buy up the riches of Germany, paid off their debts in confetti, and became staggeringly rich as a result. As part of draconian measures to aid their faltering economies, Hitler forced the merger of Germany's two major lines to create the HAPAG-Lloyd, and Mussolini consolidated Italy's three companies into Italia-Società per Azioni de Navigazione. In 1934, a beleaguered British shipping industry merged the Cunard and White Star lines, and in one fell swoop scrapped the *Majestic*, *Olympic*, *Mauretania*, *Homeric*, *Adriatic*, *Albertic*, *Doric*, and *Calgaria*. If the super-rich were still around to pay for luxury suites, the occupancy rate of normal first-, cabin-, and tourist-class accommodations plummeted, and the lines fought desperately for passengers. The CGT scrapped the *France*, and the *Ile de France* burned in port.

RESURRECTION

One of the great paradoxes of the Depression was the construction of the three largest and most expensive liners in history: the *Normandie*, *Queen Mary*, and *Queen Elizabeth*. The *Elizabeth*, however, does not really belong to the Depression; she was finished just in time to enter World War II as a troop transport. It seems bizarre that governments would finance luxury travel for the happy few while most people were struggling for a living, but there was a strange logic in their thinking. The years between the wars saw the rise of intense nationalism, and the luxury liner was a remarkable vehicle for patriotic aspirations. It simultaneously expressed power, technical prowess, and civilization. The man in the street now needed something to fuel his pride, and the construction of a supership fitted that bill perfectly. Equally important, it meant the hiring of an army of unemployed steelworkers, welders, riveters, plumbers, carpenters, painters, upholsterers, mechanics, seamen, cooks, barmen, stewards, waiters, and dishwashers. The *Normandie* and *Queen Mary* were France and Britain's equivalents to Hitler's autobahns and Roosevelt's Works Progress Adminis-

---

The Grand Salon of the *Conte di Savoia* (1931) was inspired by the Villa Borghese in Rome. Alas, the zebra-striped chairs and sofas and linoleum floors are not up to the aspirations of the frescoes or the gold-topped Corinthian pilasters. During the Depression, Mussolini merged three separate shipping companies into what became known as the Italian Line, whose flagships were the *Rex* and *Conte di Savoia*, which travelled the South Atlantic where the seas were calmer and the weather far better than on the North Atlantic run. The lavishly decorated ships had the atmosphere and trappings of cruise liners with outside pools, colorful parasols and sun-bathing passengers.

tration. Finally, one or two large ships were more economical to operate than a fleet.

The *Normandie* and *Queen Mary* were conceived at the same time, but the French proceeded with less hesitation. They suffered less from the Depression than the British did, and were more accustomed to giant government subsidies. As a result, the *Normandie* was launched a year earlier and stole the *Queen's* thunder. Statistically, the ships were quite similar. The *Normandie* measured 1,029 by 119 feet, the *Queen Mary* 1,019 by 118; the *Queen* weighed 12 percent more, but was built of heavier steel. The ships cruised practically at the same speed, and their crossing times often

varied literally by minutes. The *Normandie* took the Blue Riband on her maiden voyage with a record of four days, three hours, and two minutes, and lost it to her rival a year later when the sleek British liner beat the four-day barrier by three minutes. Both had drawbacks that were ironed out in time; the *Normandie* vibrated while the *Queen Mary* rolled. The *Mary* had far more devotees than the *Normandie*. She sailed until the sixties and still can be visited today at her pier in Long Beach, California.

The *Normandie* was undoubtedly the most elegant and comfortable ship ever to sail the seas. Every detail was the object of thoughtful planning. Naming the new liner after the French province where William the Conqueror was born was a subtle jibe at the British competition. Her massive and innovative hull was designed by an expatriate Russian engineer, Vladimir Yourkevitch. He gave her a flowing bow with semibulbous entry and rather fat thighs that eased her way through the waves. He did away with all the clutter previously placed on decks: they now became vast boulevards interconnected with elegantly curved pairs of staircases. Some 46,000 square feet of deck were turned over to the first-class passengers, and the large space between the smartly raked second and third funnels held a full-size tennis court for the first and last time on a liner. The *Normandie* was also the first ship equipped with radar. Its turboelectric propulsion made it possible for the liner to consume less fuel at twenty-nine knots than the far smaller and lighter *Ile de France* consumed at twenty-four. The miracle ship was launched in the fall of 1931, in the very depths of the Depression, to the cheers of some 200,000 people.

It took nearly two years to decorate the *Normandie*. While her technical superiority dazzled maritime buffs as well as the worried Cunard-White Star, her luxury simply could not be believed. The 1925 *Exposition des Arts Décoratifs et Industriels Modernes* inspired her public rooms. The influence of Emile-Jacques Ruhlmann, the greatest designer of the Art Deco period, was omnipresent. He only created one luxury suite and the spectacular cages in the winter garden, but his colleagues and, in some cases, disciples—including Jean Dunand, Jean Dupas, Pierre Patout, Louis Dejean, and Jan and Joël Martel—carried out his

---

A view of the famous first-class, 300-foot-long dining-room on the *Normandie*. It rose through three decks and glowed, thanks to 38 floor-to-ceiling glass appliqués, twelve light fountains and several glass chandeliers all designed by Lalique. The room was entered via a long, broad descending staircase that was a perfect vehicle for displaying wonderful couture dresses. At 14,030 cubic feet, this was the largest floating room ever created. *Opposite* A gallery on the *Queen Mary*, lined with shops, reflects the ship's poor design especially in contrast to the *Normandie*. The thin columns, barely dressed in wood, banal lighting fixtures, conventional furniture, and linoleum floors slightly helped by ugly carpets did little to glamorize what was otherwise a splendid ship.

design philosophy. The *Normandie* was predominantly a first-class ship, and 75 percent of her livable area was devoted to the comfort of 864 passengers. Every one of the 431 first-class staterooms was unique, and every conceivable decor from Louis XV to Bauhaus was employed. There were suites of spectacular luxury. The most famous were named after Normandy's fashionable resorts, Deauville and Trouville. Each had four bedrooms, a living room, dining room, pantry, servant's bedroom, five mosaic-lined bathrooms, and a large, private 675-square-foot terrace that overlooked the stern. There were adjoining rooms for personal assistants or secretaries. Sharkskin, parchment, leather,

lacquer, etched glass, and mirrors lined the walls; superb Art Deco macassar furniture upholstered in specially woven Beauvais tapestry filled the interior space; and a white piano enlivened the cocktail hour. Jules Leleu and Louis Süe decorated the Art Deco Trouville and Deauville suites, respectively, while the more staid Jansen and Carlhin, among others, tackled the suites inspired by an earlier period.

The ship's tone was established as soon as passengers got off the gangplank and entered the two-and-a-half-deck-high main embarkation hall lined in cream-colored Algerian onyx and presided over by a large cloisonné knight in armor. At the end of the hall a pair

A drawing of the *Normandie*'s Grand Salon by Jean Pages. The centerpiece of a great

defile of rooms that crossed uninterrupted for 700 feet through the promenade deck,

the grand salon was the highest room ever built on an ocean liner. It was punctuated by

six circular settees, upholstered in Aubusson tapestry, and its rug could be lifted for

dancing. The walls were sheathed by Jean Dupas in glass panels etched in gold, silver,

platinum and palladium devoted to the history of navigation.

of twenty-foot bronze doré doors by Raymond Subes opened up to the ship's most famous room, the first-class *Salle à Manger*, which was presided over by the head steward in white tie and tails. The enormous inside room rose through three decks, its three-hundred-foot length enhanced by its relative narrowness; the space cut right through the center of the ship, leaving the outside free for portholed staterooms. Although there was no natural light, the room glowed thanks to thirty-eight floor-to-ceiling glass and gold *appliques* and twelve large illuminated-glass fountains designed by René Lalique. There were eight secluded private rooms for small dinner parties and one banquet room. Diners were kept comfortably cool by one of the earliest and certainly the largest air-conditioning units yet installed on a liner.

The final public rooms on this deck were a small writing room and a bookless library, attached to an amazing winter garden lined with trellises on which orchids and other tropical plants grew. Water bubbled out of fountains as birds twittered in two immense Ruhlmann crystal and bronze cages. This semicircular

tropical paradise let in the sun from a series of large windows that covered the entire perimeter of the room and looked over the bow at the ship's seemingly endless wake.

The *Queen Mary*, although less glamorous, reigned over the Atlantic with the *Queen Elizabeth*, her sister ship, in the postwar years. For those who had never known the *Normandie*, the *Mary* was impressively elegant. Her cabins were comfortable and her public rooms enormous. Unfortunately, her decoration was stodgy and middle class. Exotic woods were used instead of coromandel lacquer and glass, and passengers felt a bit like flies in a honey pot. The floors were mostly linoleum, Formica covered the tables, the stuffed chairs were unattractive, and the patterned carpets even worse. In a way, the *Queen* was like an overblown Art Deco private yacht and simply had no panache. Alas, at the time Britain was simply not blessed with a great school of design. On the other hand, the crew mixed dignity with kindness and passengers felt as if they were spending the weekend in a grand country house where one had to watch one's manners. But the *Queen Mary* was a real ship, and one felt a long and distinguished nautical past in every rivet. And—most important—the American clientele felt secure speaking English. A Danish observer pinpointed the main difference between the rivals: "The French," he wrote, "have built a beautiful hotel and

Below The *Normandie*'s grand salon was the social center of the ship and used for all sorts of entertainments. Here, acrobats perform after the inaugural dinner in Le Havre. One of Lalique's eight fountains parallels the acrobats; these fountains, along with metal urns that cast light upwards, were part of the wonderful illumination that inspired passengers to refer to the *Normandie* as "the ship of lights." *Above* The first class dining-room of the *Queen Mary* was a symphony of precious woods. The decorative wall panel allowed the passengers to follow the ship's progress. The fashionable place to dine, however, was the Verandah grill from whose bay windows diners could watch the wake of the ship stretching into the distance.

put a ship around it. The British have built a beautiful ship and put a hotel inside it."

TWILIGHT

Charles Lindbergh tolled the death knell for the great transatlantic liners in 1927. That year, the CGT installed a mail plane on the *Ile de France*, which was catapulted off the deck a day before the ship reached port. This was a rather pointless exercise, but got a lot of publicity and always entertained the passengers. A year later, the Germans capitalized on the experience they had gained in World War I, and launched the first commercial dirigible, the *Graf Zeppelin*. In a decade of service, it carried 18,000 passengers between Frankfurt and Rio, traveling a million miles without an accident.

In 1933, the Boeing 247 was introduced as the first commercial airplane, and by 1936 American Airlines introduced the DC-3, which carried twenty-one passengers between New York and Chicago. Commercial aviation was hesitantly launched in Europe, and the daring Maharaja of Jaipur flew from his polo field to London with multiple stops over a period of nine days.

In May 1936, Germany sent up the *Hindenburg*. The cigar-shaped airship, filled with 7,200,000 cubic feet of hydrogen, could lift a gross weight of 236 tons, and could cruise continuously at eighty miles per hour for five or six days. New York could be reached from Frankfurt in sixty hours while the Bishop's Rock to Ambrose Point sea course took four days. Adding on the time from Bremen to Bishop's Rock, this meant that the liners' crossing time had effectively been cut in two. The Depression was not the only shadow on the

Above **The observation platform of the *Hindenburg* just off the main lounge of the airship. The living quarters were**

slung under the belly of the gigantic dirigible, and were a self-contained world including 25 staterooms, each with a

toilet and hot and cold running water (*opposite below left*). The staterooms were copied after those on Pullman cars

and were comfortable enough for the two nights needed to cross the ocean. From the solid wall of windows,

passengers could watch the green fields below. Note the flimsy but durable Bauhaus furniture; the aluminum chairs

were so light that they could be lifted with two fingers.

horizon of the shipping world! And the *Hindenburg* was exceedingly comfortable, since it copied many features of the luxury liner. Slung onto her belly was a self-contained world with twenty-five staterooms, each with a toilet and hot and cold running water. These small compartments were copied after those on Pullman cars, and were quite comfortable for the two nights needed to cross. There was a lounge with sturdy aluminum chairs so light that they could be lifted with two fingers, and a dining room lit by a solid wall of windows from which one could watch the green fields or ocean below. The airship had a spiffy crew dressed in white jackets with gold buttons. A large swastika was glued on to her immense rudder. It looked as if the zeppelin was the wave of the future until the *Hindenburg* suddenly exploded, probably in an act of sabotage, on May 6, 1937, just as she was about to moor at Lakehurst, New Jersey. The ship was close to the ground and many of the passengers and crew jumped to safety, but others were incinerated. Sympathy for the victims was mitigated by delight in a colossal propaganda defeat for Nazi Germany.

Queen Elizabeth launched her namesake on September 27, 1938, just as Hitler prepared to invade Czechoslovakia. It was hardly a festive occasion, and

Above The *Hindenburg* in flames in 1937 in Lakehurst, New Jersey. This terrible accident, quite possibly an act of sabotage, spelled the end of the dirigible as an alternative form of transatlantic crossing. It also created a conception of the dirigible as a dangerous form of transportation, which was in fact not the case. *Below right* Passengers embark on the Pan American *Clipper.*

Chamberlain flew to Munich to appease the great dictator. He returned on October 1 to announce "peace in our time." In August 1939, Ribbentrop flew to Moscow to make his pact with Stalin and the die was cast. On September 1, 1939, Nazi Germany invaded Poland and war was declared. This time the Germans made sure that none of their liners was stuck in New York's neutral harbor. The *Normandie* arrived on August 28 and never saw France again. Placed under the control of the U.S. Navy for transformation into a troopship, a careless worker cutting down one of Lalique's light fountains in the Grand Salon sprayed sparks from an acetylene torch onto a bundle of tar-coated kapok and started a fire that soon engulfed the ship. It was possibly sabotage, and the ship might have been saved if it had not been for the incompetence and

overzealousness of her American guardians. She was totally flooded by fire fighters and eventually rolled onto her side, an irreparable and embarrassing hulk.

World War II and the death of the *Normandie* marked the end of the golden age of travel. As the Atlantic filled with submarines, Pan Am sent its comfortable flying clippers from Lisbon to New York. The Duke of Windsor, with his duchess and pugs, was airborne to New York and on to govern Nassau. With Europe in flames and the ex-king of England ruling a coral reef with a Baltimore divorcée, the old order had now very clearly come to an end. Once the terrible conflict had finished, liners still crossed the seas and luxury trains made their way across the tracks. The stars were in the sky, but this time they were on airplanes.

Above Transatlantic flights became a serious alternative to crossing by liner just before World War II,

and, during the war, the Pam Am *Flying Clipper* from Lisbon to New York was a far safer means of

travel than zigzagging across the ocean to avoid U-boats. In a curious way, these slow planes were far

more comfortable than today's, as can be confirmed by the glamorous lady (*opposite*), preparing for

bed on an American Airlines flight in the 1930s. Double bunks lined the first-class section of

transatlantic planes through the 1950s, and the top section was folded up during the day.

W EPILOGUE

When rich and titled gentlemen got together in the Belle Epoque, they generally discussed their mistresses and horses. Between the wars, as society became more heavily weighted toward the rich rather than the aristocratic, they talked about their business. Today, the main conversational topic of the super-rich is private planes. They drone on endlessly about the differences between a Gulf Stream, a 707, or a Mystère 20, discussing speed, gas consumption, safety, and flight span. The private jet has become the equivalent of the private railroad car, but with one main difference: the private car was generally attached to a public train, even if the whole train made special stops for the convenience of its few rich passengers. The private jet is, literally, free as a bird, and in this it reflects the change of true luxury travel from the public display of wealth to a much more private world of superluxe.

The grand hotels are still with us and—in a way—are more comfortable than they were. The Ritz hotels of London, Paris, and Madrid have been taken over by conscientious owners who have modernized them and introduced gadgetry and fixtures that would have thrilled the most spoiled or demanding traveler of the Belle Epoque. The splendidly restored Hôtel de Paris, in Monte Carlo, is as beautiful as ever, and the same could be said of the Brenner's Park in Baden-Baden or the Palace Hotel in Saint Moritz. Their only problem is that, instead of being a gathering place for the elegant and fashionable of this world—of which there are still many—they are filled with the simply rich or businessmen on an expense account. Balance sheets, rather than racing forms, blanket the tables, and the attaché case has replaced the hatbox or leather jewelry case. One of the last holdouts is Claridge's in London, still filled with royals and heads of state; until very recently the bills were written out by hand.

Real *luxe* has gone private, and it is in luxurious villas that the gilded traveler generally is to be found. The question today is not *where* you stay, but *with whom*. The prize invitations in the South of France come from the Harding Laurences of Texas and New York, Paul-Louis Weiller at the Reine Jeanne near Hyères, or the David-Weills at Cap d'Antibes. In Saint Moritz, it is the Agnellis, Stavros Niarchos, or George Livanos; in Gstaad Valentino, the William Buckleys, or the Roger Moores. Neither the hosts nor the guests are ever seen in a hotel, and if they go to a restaurant the whole place has generally been taken for the evening. The epitome of *luxe* is now the private island, particularly in the Aegean, where Greek shipping tycoons such as Stavros Niarchos ferry in guests and caviar on fleets of helicopters. The sky is so filled with them around the island of Spetsai that the ordinary traveler has trouble closing an eye. Today's fashionable guests generally expect not only room and board but free transport as well. This is no problem for the likes of Donald Trump or the Forbes family, who have their own 707s to bring people in from New York and Paris to their celebrity parties. Great yachts still exist, probably in more ample supply than ever, although there are not too many three hundred footers left. But Niarchos's *Atlantis* or Trump's *Princess* surpass the dreams of earlier yachtsmen. In the summer the yachts are berthed cheek by jowl in such fashionable ports as Monte Carlo, Cannes, Porto Cervo, Portofino, or Vouliagmeni, and pretty coves on the Turkish coast fill up at night with floating palaces whose sailors pollute the waters with the garbage of their spoiled and indifferent owners. It would, however, be difficult today to find a sailing boat with such stylish passengers as the Duke of Westminster and his mistress Coco Chanel, who tossed a priceless emerald necklace into the sea on the pretext that she could not be bought for a few stones.

Liners exist, although they are now most often cruise ships filled with passengers who are cut off from any interest except saving taxes and rewriting their last will and testament. An expression of the longing for privacy are the small liners *Sea Goddess I* and *II*, with space for less than a hundred passengers, which have been chartered on rare occasions. A British heiress took one over for a ten-day cruise to celebrate her fiftieth birthday. Her guests were brought to Venice by a chartered plane to find the lovely ship waiting for them off the

Opposite The *Liberté* sails into the French Line's New York dock. This lovely ship was none other than North German Lloyd's *Europa*, which had been launched in 1929 and was the sister ship of the *Bremen*. The French seized her after World War II from a defeated Germany, just as the British and Americans had seized the bulk of Germany's merchant marine at the declaration of World War I.

Doge's Palace, an orchestra was flown in from New York, the guests were seated for meals by computer to avoid monotony and misunderstandings, and smaller jets flew people in and out as the champagne-filled ship made her way to Turkey. There were even rumors that the ship had a submarine following in its wake to protect her from terrorists. In an equally luxurious vein, the late bon vivant Malcolm Forbes took his pals down the mosquito- and piranha-infested Amazon in his air-conditioned *Highlander*, and Ann Getty hired a beautiful felucca to take thirty friends up the Nile.

In some ways, travel today is more luxurious than it was, and certainly easier and more varied, since planes and hotel chains have made the most exotic outposts accessible. The average traveler today name-drops such odd destinations as Katmandu, the Seychelles, Phuket, Easter Island, Tonga, or Bali. Sadly, however, convenience has imposed a certain homogenization, and travel has lost much of its adventure. And, to a great degree, it has lost most of its glamour, except for a very few of the super-rich or well-born. It is my hope that the many entertaining photographs in this book, as well as some of its reminiscences, have brought back for a few ephemeral hours the fun of a lost way of life.

The funnels of the *France*.

ACKNOWLEDGEMENTS

The Golden Age of Travel covers a vast territory over a fairly long period of time, and would have been impossible to write without reference to a great many books. These range from contemporary travel experiences to compilations. From some of these wells I have drawn buckets, from others merely a glassful, and I shall always regret the amount of remarkable information I have been obliged to omit. I should particularly like to acknowledge the many books on luxury trains by George Behrend; Christopher Hibbert's recreation of the Grand Tour; Lucius Beebe on private trains and American tycoons; John Malcom Brenner and John Maxtone-Graham on ocean liners; Marc and Catherine Walter for their books on grand hotels and casinos throughout the world; John Rousmaniere and the editors at Time-Life for their splendid book on luxury yachts; Amelia Edwards for her record of Egypt in the 19th Century, and Leonard Cottrell for his in the 20th; Michael Shoemaker for his splendid work on the Trans-Siberian Railroad; Boris Ometev and John Stuart for Saint Petersburg; and, of course, the timeless Mr. Baedeker. The personal reminiscences of Her Highness the Raj Mata of Jaipur on Royal India; Mrs. John Barry Ryan on travel with her father, Otto Kahn; and Prince Naguib Abdallah on life in the palmy days of Egypt under the Khedive were all priceless. My thanks also go to Joanne Polster for her help in library research and to Bernice Gelzer, without whose computer mastery descriptions of Siberia would be side to side with winter life in Palm Beach. My special thanks, also, to the publishers and editors involved in the different editions of the book: David Campbell, François Robichon, Christopher Fagg and Anness Law for assistance on the English language edition.

BIBLIOGRAPHY

About (Edmond), *De Pontoise à Constantinople*, Paris, Hachette, 1884.

Amory (Cleveland), *The Last Resorts*. New York, Harper, 1952.

Anderson (Roy), *White Star*, Prescot, Lancashire, T. Stephenson, 1964.

Andrews (Wayne), *The Vanderbilt Legend*. New York, Harcourt, Brace & Company, 1941.

Ardman (Harvey), *Normandy: Her Life and Times*, Franklin Watts, 1985.

Aylmer (Gerald), *R.M.S. Mauretania: The Ship and Her Record*. London, P. Marshall and Company Ltd, 1935.

Baedeker (Karl), *Austria-Hungary Including Dalmatia and Bosnia*. Leipzig, Karl Baedeker, 1905. *Russia: A Handbook for Travellers*. New York, Arno Press, 1971. Reprint of 1914 edition.

Barbance (Marthe), *Histoire de la Compagnie Générale Transatlantique: un siècle d'exploitation maritime*. Paris, Arts et Métiers Graphiques, 1955.

Barber (Noel), *Trans Siberian*, London, 1942.

Barsley (Michael), *The Orient Express*. New York, Stein and Day, 1966.

Bates (Lindon, Jr), *The Russia Road to China*, Boston, Houghton Mifflin Company, 1910.

Beaton (Cecil), *The Glass of Fashion*. London, Weidenfeld & Nicolson, 1954.

Beebe (Lucius), *Mansions on Rails; The Folklore of the Private Railway Car*. Berkeley, CA, Howell-North, 1959. *Mr. Pullman's Elegant Palace Car*. Garden City, NY, Doubleday, 1961. *The Big Spenders*. Garden City, NY, Doubleday, 1966.

Behrend (George), *Luxury Trains from the Orient Express to TGV*. New York, Vendôme Press, 1982. *The History of Wagons-Lits 1875–1955*. London, Modern Transport Publishing Company, 1959.

Behrman (S. N.), *Duveen*. New York, Random House, 1952.

Belzoni (Giovanni Battista), *Narrative of the Operations and Recent Discoveries . . . in Egypt and Nubia*. London, J. Murray, 1821.

Benson (Edward Frederic), *King Edward VII.*
London, Longmans, Green and Company, 1933

Berg (Lev Semionovich), *Les Régions Naturelles de l'URSS*. Traduction française de G. Welter, Paris, Payot, 1941.

Bibesco (Princesse), *Jour d'Egypte*. Paris, Flammarion, 1929.

Billings (Henry), *Superliners S.S. United States*. New York, Viking Press, 1953.

Blowitz (Henri), *Une Course à Constantinople*. Paris, E. Plon, 1884.

Bonsall (Thomas E.), *The Titanic*. New York, Gallery Books, W. H. Smith Publishers, 1987.

Brander (Bruce), *The River Nile*. Washington, D.C., The National Geographic Society, 1966.

Brinnin (John Malcolm), *Grand Luxe Transatlantic Style*. New York, Holt, Rinehart, Winston, 1986. *The Sway of the Grand Saloon*. New York, Delacorte Press, 1971.

Brown (Arthur Judson), *The Mastery of the Far East*, New York, Charles Scribner's Sons, 1919.

Burton (Lady Isabel Arundlell), *The Inner Life of Syria, Palestine and the Holy Land*. London, H. S. King and Company, 1875.

Butler (Alfred J.), *Court Life in Egypt*. London, Chapman & Hall, 1887.

Carco (Francis), *Palace d'Egypte*. Paris, 1933.

Carter (Howard and A. C. Mace), *The Tomb of Tut Anh Amen*. London, Cassell and Company Ltd, 1923–27.

Cecil (Lamar), *Albert Ballin: Business and Politics in Imperial Germany, 1888—1918*. Princeton, Princeton University Press, 1967.

Channing (C. G. Fairfax), *Siberia's Untouched Treasure*. New York, G. P. Putnam's Sons, 1923.

Collins (Perry McDonough), *A Voyage Down the Amoor*. New York, D. Appleton and Company, 1860.

Commault (R.), *Georges Nagelmackers*. Paris, 1966.

Corey (Lewis), *The House of Morgan*. New York, G. H. Watt, 1930.

Cottrell (Leonard), *Egypt*. New York, Oxford University Press, 1966.

Cowles (Virginia), *Edward VII and His Circle*. London, Hamish Hamilton, 1956.

Daney (Charles), *Le Transsiberien*. Paris, Herscher, 1980.

Davey (Richard), *The Sultan and His Subjects*. London, Chapman and Hall, 1897.

Daye (Pierre), *Leopold II*. Paris, A. Fayard, 1934.

Dekobra (Maurice), *La Madonne des Sleepings*. Paris, 1925.

Dethin (Jean), *Gares d'Europe*. Paris, Denoel, 1987.

Dewindt (Harry), *Siberia As It Is*. London, Chapman and Hall, 1892.

Edwards (Amelia B.), *A Thousand Miles up the Niles*. London, G. Routledge & Sons, 1889.

Ellis (Cuthbert Hamilton), *Royal Trains*. London, Routledge and Kegan Paul, 1975.

Frost (Wesley), *German Submarine Wafare*. New York, D. Appleton and Company, 1918.

Gautier (Théophile), *Voyage en Russie*. Paris, 1966.

Goethe (Johann Wolfgang von), *Italian Journey; 1786–1788*. Translated into english by W. H. Auden and Elizabeth Mayer. New York, Pantheon Books, 1962.

Grant (Kay), *Samuel Cunard*. London Abelard-Schuman, 1967.

The Graphic: An Illustrated Newspaper. London, 8 June 1907.

Greene (Graham), *Stamboul Train*. London, Heinemann, 1959.

Gregory (Alexis et al.), *Grand American Hotels*. New York, Vendôme Press, 1989.

Guillet (Edwin Clarence), *The Great Migration; The Atlantic Crossing by Sailing Ship Since 1770*. Toronto, T. Nelson & Sons, 1937.

Halsband (Robert), *The Complete Letters of Lady Mary Wortley Montague*. Oxford, Clarendon Press, 1965–67.

Herling (Albert Conrad), *The Soviet Slave Empire*. New York, Wilfred Funk, 1951.

Hibbert (Christopher), *Grand Tour*. New York, Putnam, 1969.

Heckstall-Smith (Antony), *Sacred Cowes or The Cream of Yachting Society*. London, A. Wingate, 1955.

Husband (Joseph), *The Story of the Pullman Car*. Chicago, A. C. McClurg & Company, 1917.

Kavaler (Lucy), *The Astors*. New York, Dodd, Mead, 1966.

Laver (James), *Edwardian Promenade*. Boston, Houghton Mifflin Company, 1958.

Lee (Charles E.), *The Blue Riband: The Romance of the Atlantic Ferry*. London, S. Low, Marston & Company Ltd, 1930.

Lehmen (Ernst A.), *Zeppelin: The Story of Lighter-Than-Air Craft*. London, Longmans, Green, 1937.

Lewis (Wilmarth), *The Yale Edition of Horace Walpole's Correspondence*. New Haven, Yale University Press, 1937.

Lichtervelde (Comte Louis de), *Leopold of the Belgians*. New York, The Century Company, 1929. Translated into English by Thomas H. and H. Russell Reed.

Lord (Walter), *A Night to Remember*. New York, Holt, Rinehart & Winston, 1955.

Maspero (Gaston), *Les Momies Royales de Dér el-Bahari*. Cairo, Institut Français d'Archéologie Orientale, *Mémoire de la Mission du Caire*, Vol. 1, fasc. 4 (1887), pp 511–787.

Massie (Robert K.), *Nicholas and Alexandra*. New York, Atheneum, 1967.

Massingham (Hugh and Pauline). *The Englishman Abroad*. London, Phoenix House, 1962.

Maurois (André), *Edouard VII et son temps*. Paris, Les Editions de France, 1933.

Maxtone-Graham (John), *The Only Way to Cross*. New York, Macmillan, 1972.

Mead (William Edward), *The Grand Tour in the Eighteenth-Century*. Boston, Houghton Mifflin Company, 1914.

Meade (Martin), *Grand Oriental Hotels*. London, Dent, 1987.

Myers (Gustavus), *The History of Great American Fortunes*. New York, The Modern Library, 1937.

Mooney (Michael), *The Hindenburg*. New York, Dodd, Mead, 1972.

Moore (George Greville), *Society Recollections in Paris and Vienna: 1879–1904*. New York, D. Appleton and Company, 1908.

Morton (Frederic), *The Rothschilds*. New York, Atheneum, 1962.

Noble (Celia Brunel), *The Brunels, Father and Son*. London, Cobden-Sanderson, 1939.

Normandie, *Le Géant des Mers*. Paris, Herscher, 1985.

Pares (Sir Bernard), *The Fall of The Russian Monarchy*. London, J. Cape, 1939.

Parks (George Bruner), *The English Traveler to Italy*. Stamford, CA, Stamford University Press, 1954.

Pecheux (Julien), *Age d'Or du Rail Européen*. Paris, Berger Levrault, 1975.

Pudney (John), *The Thomas Cook Story*. London, M. Joseph, 1953.

Quennell (Peter), *Byron in Italy*. New York, Viking Press, 1941.

Rey (J.), *The Whole Art of Dining*. London, Carmona & Baker, 1920.

Ritz (Marie Louise), *César Ritz. Host to the World*. London, 1938.

Rolt (Lionel Thomas Caswell), *Isambard Kingdom Brunel: A Biography*. London, Longmans, Green, 1957.

Rousmaniere (John), *The Luxury Yachts*. Alexandria, VA, Time-Life Books, 1981.

Sackville-West (Victoria), *The Edwardians*. Garden City, NY, Doubleday, Doran, 1930.

Salisbury (Harrison E.), *To Moscow and Beyond*. New York, Harper, 1960.

Shoemaker (Michael Myers), *The Great Siberian Railway*. New York, G. P. Putnam's Sons, 1903.

Sitwell (Sacheverell), *Roumanian Journey*. New York, Charles Scribner's Sons, 1938.

Spratt (H. Philip), *Transatlantic Paddle Steamers*. Glasgow, Brown, Son and Ferguson, 1951.

Steegmuller (Francis), *Flaubert in Egypt*. Boston, Little Brown, 1972.

Swinglehurt (Edmund), *The Romantic Journey: The Story of Thomas Cook and Victorian Travel*. New York, Harper and Row, 1975.

Theroux (Paul), *The Great Railway Bazaar: By Train Through Asia*. Boston, Houghton Mifflin Company, 1975.

Toland (John), *Ships in the Sky: The Story of the Great Dirigibles*. New York, Holt, 1957.

Tupper (Harmon), *To the Great Ocean: Siberia and the Trans-Siberian Railway*. Boston, Little, Brown, 1965.

Twain (Mark), *Innocents Abroad*. Hartford, CT, American Publishing Company, 1869.

Villes d'Eau en France Paris, IFA, 1985.

Waldeck (R. G.), *Athene Palace*. New York, Robert McBride and Company, 1942.

Wall (Robert), *Ocean Liners*. London, Collins, 1980. (Also New York, E. P. Dutton, 1977.)

Wechsberg (Joseph), *Lost World of the Great Spas*. New York, Harper and Row, 1979.

Winter (C. W. R.), *Queen Mary: Her Early Years Recalled*. New York, W. W. Norton, 1986.

PHOTOGRAPHIC CREDITS AND ACKNOWLEDGEMENTS

Archiv für Kunst und Geschichte Berlin: 22 (top), 162, 185, 192 (bottom), 205. Asprey, London: 14. Baden-Baden Stadtmuseum: 37 (top). Bettmann Archive, New York: 10, 16, 18 (centre), 19, 20, 29, 46 (top and bottom), 47, 49, 50, 51, 60, 62, 63, 64 (bottom), 67 (bottom), 69, 174, 180 (top), 181 (top), 184, 186, 187, 188, 192 (bottom), 195 (centre), 197, 209, 213 (top right), 214, 216. Bibliothèque Forney, Paris: 84, 160, 195 (bottom). Bowron Studios, New York: 206. Cahiers du Cinéma: 207, J. Calmann & King, London: 145. Chevojon: 15 (bottom), 90, 171, Cinémathèque français: 118 (bottom). Compagnie des Wagons-Lits: 46 (centre), 52 (top), 55, 56, 58, 88, 98 (bottom), 114, 115, 116, 117 (bottom), 118 (bottom), 119, 120, 121, 122, 123, 124, 128 (bottom and centre), 129 (bottom), 131, 132 (bottom), 134, (bottom), 141 (top), 147 (bottom), 148, 150, 151, 154, 164, 215. Thomas Cook & Sons, London: 13, 101 (centre), 112 (top), 153, 158 (bottom), 159, 168. Christies, London: 32. Deutsches Museum, Munich: 213 (top left). Michel Doerr: 138/139. Dunedin Art Gallery, New Zealand: 40. Ecole Nationale des Ponts et Chaussées: 43. Edimedia: 68, 70/71 (Snark), 73 (bottom). Giraudon: 24/25 (Bridgeman), 89 (Musée de Petit Palais), 107 (Bridgeman), 111, 169 (Bridgeman), 170 (Bridgeman). Lise Grenier: 30, 31. Hapag-Lloyd A. G. Hambourg: 172, 173, 189, 193 (bottom), 204. Lewis H. Hine: 190. Hulton Deutsch Collection, London: 9, 17, 18 (bottom), 22 (top), 26, 27, 75 (top), 158 (top), 165, 181 (top), 199 (right), 202. L'Illustration/Sygma: 42, 44, 53, 72, 175, 194 (bottom), 198, 201 (bottom), 208. Luftschiffbau Zepelin Gmbh: 212, 213 (bottom). J. Massey Stewart, London: 139, 143, 144. Ministère de la Culture, Paris/photo F. Kollar: 11. Musée des Arts décoratifs, Paris/photo Sully-Jeaulmes: 82. Musée d'Orsay, Paris/photo Alfred Stieglitz: 191. Musée de la Publicité, Paris: 91 (bottom). Musée Romboli-train, Rambouillet: 136/137. New York Public Library: 34, 194 (bottom). A. P. Novosti: 147 (bottom), 149. Owen Edgar Gallery, London: 8, P & O, London: 176 (top), 182/183. Popperfoto, London: 64 (top), 75 (top), 101 (top), 117 (bottom), 125 (bottom), 180 (bottom), 211 (top). Public Record Office, Crown Copyright, cover. Roger-Viollet: 23, 32, 35, 36, 38, 87, 91 (top), 93, 103, 104 (top), 125, (top), 126, 127, (top), 128 (top), 141, 142, 156, (bottom), 176 (centre), 195 (top), 199 (left), 217. Royal Commonwealth Society, London: 1, 2/3, 4/5, 6/7, 65, 66. Sirot-Angel: 45, 52 (top), 74, 129 (top), 135, 146, 178/179. Société de Géographic, Paris: 150. La Vie Rail: 59, 140. Louis Vuitton A. A.: 21, 137, 176 (top), 177, Coll. Walter: 12, 15, 18 (top), 20, 37 (top), 39, 41, 54, 67 (bottom), 73 (top), 76, 77, 78, 79, 80, 81, 83, 85, 92, 94, 95, 96/97, 98 (top), 99 (bottom), 100, 101 (bottom), 102, 104 (bottom), 105, 106, 108, 109, 110, 112 (bottom), 113, 127 (top), 130, 132 (top), 133, 134 (top), 152, 155, 156 (top), 157, 161, 163, 166, 167, 193 (bottom). Droits réservés: 48, 91 (bottom), 196, 200/201, 210, 211 (bottom).